James LaFond

Masculine Axis

A Meditation on Manhood and Heroism

Dust cover

James LaFond writes about masculinity with the assurance of a man who knows what he is about. Only by understanding and practicing masculinity, through literature, at work, with their mates and family members, in combat, sports and in fellowship with other men, may the men of our sick society preserve their property, families, cultural patrimony and their own souls.

A Punch Buggy Book

www.jameslafond.com

jameslafond.blogspot.com

Cover art, foreword and editing by Lynn Lockhart.

Foreword

The Masculine Axis is the center; the center of gravity, the axis of rotation, the polar reference of the world we live in. James LaFond knows this. He may have been born knowing it, but he also knows it through his uncommonly deeply lived life, and he wants to share it with you before it slips irretrievably away. LaFond has lived perhaps a half-dozen lifetimes during the fifty-odd years he has clocked on his earthly coil: a lifetime in combat, a lifetime in urban survival, a lifetime in the grocery business, fatherhood, one marriage and assorted Khanish dalliances, several lifetimes worth of books published, even a scholastic one spent in libraries learning ancient Greek, reading the texts of the major religions, and I'm sure I have missed a few others.

Read this book, learn about masculinity, if you are a man, practice it in your own life, if you are a woman, seek it in your mate, nurture it in your sons, and teach your daughters the same.

Thank you, James, for the chance to contribute.

Lynn Lockhart

Books by James LaFond

Nonfiction

The Fighting Edge, 2000
The Logic of Steel, 2001
The First Boxers, 2011
The Gods of Boxing, 2011
All Power Fighting, 2011
When You're Food, 2011
The Lesser Angles of Our Nature, 2012
The Logic of Force, 2012
The Greatest Boxer, 2012
Take Me to Your Breeder, 2014
The Streets Have Eyes, 2014
Panhandler Nation, 2014
The Ghetto Grocer, 2014
American Fist, 2014
Don't Get Boned, 2014
Alienation Nation, 2014
In The Chinks of The Machine, 2014
How the Ghetto Got My Soul, 2014
Saving the World Sucks, 2014
Taboo You, 2014
Taboo You Man Cave Edition, 2014
Letters from Planet Meathead, 2014
Shorn of Little Sissy Thins, 2014
Winter of a Fighting Life, 2014
Narco Night Train, 2014
Into the Mountains of Madness: in [3 volumes], 2014
Incubus of Your Sacred Emasculation, 2014
Breeder's Digest, 2014
The Third Eye, 2015
Modern Agonistics, 2015
By the Wine Dark Sea, 2015
At the End of Masculine Time, 2015
War Drums, 2015
A Thousand Years in His Soul: The Poets, 2015

Masculine Axis

A Thousand Years in His Soul: The Seers, 2015
The GQ Mugging Inquest, 2015
Of Lions and Men, 2015
Your Trojan Whorse, 2016
On Bitches, 2016
Equidistant Drowning Babies, 2015
The Boned Zone, 2015
A Sickness of the Heart: Part One, 2015
Let the Weak Fall, 2015
If I Were King, 2015
Dark Art of an Aryan Mystic, 2015
Welcome to Harm City: White Boy, 2015
When You're Food: Raw, 2016
The Punishing Art, 2016
Twerps, Goons and Meatshields, 2016
Our Captain, 2016
Stillbirth of a Nation, 2016
America in Chains, 2106
40,000 Years from Home, 2016
The Sardonyx Stone, 2017
Paleface Sunset, 2016
Habitat Hoodrat: Ho Nation, 2016
A Once Great Medieval City, 2016
Right on White Time, 2016
A Well of Heroes: One, 2016
Thriving in Bad Places, 2016
Into Wicked Company, 2016
One Soul Under God, 2016
Under the God of Things, 2016
When Your Job Sucks, 2016
Dawn in Dindustan, 2017
Good Morning Dindustan, 2017
White in the Savage Night, 2017
A Well of Heroes: Two, 2017
The Hunt for Whitey, 2017
Habitat Hoodrat: Yo Nation, 2017
Rubbing Out Palefaces, 2017

A Bright Shining Lie at Dusk, 2017
The Lies that Bind Us, 2017
Being a Bad Man in a Worse World, 2017
So That His Master May Have Him Again, 2017
So That Her Master May Have Her Again, 2017
The Pale Usher, 2017
Masculine Axis, 2017
Writing Unchained, 2017
Man Gearing, 2018
Why Grownups Suck, 2018
A Dread Grace, 2018
A Well of Heroes: Three, 2018
The Boxer Dread, 2018
Aryan Myth, 2018
Against the Golden Race, 2018
Magic Dindus and White Devils, 2018
The Last Whiteman in Baltimore, 2018
The Vile Root, 2018

Fiction

Astride the Chariot of Night, 2014
Sacrifix, 2014
Rise, 2014
Motherworld, 2014
Planet Buzzkill, 2014
Fruit of The Deceiver, 2014
Forty Hands of Night, 2014
Black and Pale, 2014
Daughters of Moros, 2014
Darkly, 2014
This Design is Called Paisley, 2015
Hurt Stoker, 2015
Poet, 2016
Triumph, 2015
Winter, 2015
RetroGenesis: Day 1, with Erique Watson, 2015
Easy Chair, 2015

Happily Ever Under, 2015
Road Killing, 2015
Fat Girl Dancing, 2015
Buzz Bunny, 2015
T. Spoone Slickens, Inquire, 2015
Dream Flower, 2015
Organa, 2015
A Hoodrat Halloween, 2015
Menthol Rampage, 2015
The Consultant, 2015
Reverent Chandler, 2015
He, 2016
Little Feet Going Nowhere, 2016
DoomFawn, 2016
Hemavore, with S. L. James, 2016
The Jericho Bone, 2016
Ire and Ice, 2016
Night City, 2016
Skulker Jones, 2016
A White Christmas, 2016
Malediction Song, 2017
Drink Deep of Night, 2017
The Spiral Case, 2017
Yusef of the Dusk, 2017
Wendigo, 2017
Sold, 2017
Beyond the Pale, 2018
Bad Medicine, 2018
NightSong of the Nords, 2018
The Absolvant, 2018
The Filthy Few [with Samuel Finlay], 2018
Kettle of Bones, 2019

Sunset Saga Novels
Big Water Blood Song, 2011
Ghosts of the Sunset World, 2011
Beyond the Ember Star, 2012

Comes the Six Winter Night, 2012
Thunder-Boy, 2012
The World is Our Widow, 2013
Behind the Sunset Veil, 2013
Den of the Ender, 2013
God's Picture Maker, 2014
Out of Time, 2015
Seven Moons Deep, 2017
WhiteSkyCanoe, 2018

Available exclusively at www.jameslafond.com/store:

Nonfiction
All Power Fighting, 2011
Predation, 2012
The Broken Dance, 2012

Fiction
Soter's Way, 2012
Sunset Saga: Pillagers of Time, 2012
By This Axe!, 2012
God of War, 2013
Riding the Nightmare, 2013
Triumph, 2015

Contents

Masculine Axis

For Scott Nehring, an unlikely friend whom Wicked Fate pushed unexpectedly my way

All thanks to Lynn Lockhart for taking the interest and time to shape this work into something much better than it might have otherwise been.

Thanks to Baruch Kogan, Jeremy Bentham, Bob Jones, Ishmael, Steevo, Adam and Julian for their well-considered contributions.

-Friday, September 1, 2017

The Masculine Axis

Where would a sigma fit into this hierarchy? A Man Question from Lazer

January 13, 2017

Reader Lazer asks where a sigma would fit into the hierarchy of masculine roles described in *Drinking Companion Personality Characteristics,* comprising Alpha, Beta and Omega males.

Lazer, thanks for the opportunity to explain this concept, something I find I have neglected, and continue to illustrate through mythic, historical, sports, survival, and workplace examples.

To begin with let me separate myself from Huxley's use of the Hellenic alphabet in *Brave New World,* a book I enjoyed and a concept that I think is being pushed upon us, but which is off the mark for our purposes. When discussing the masculine axis, neo-tribalists are prone to stress hierarchy, with every man looking ahead and ascending the linear staircase to masculine realization in accordance to his merit in the hierarchy. But that is hardly realistic is it?

Primal tribal structures—in every example I have studied—have also had a minority of set aside types, the shamanic type for instance.

Imagine a family in which grandpa gets to the point where he hands over the business to his son, but remains as an advisor, no longer a leader, no longer the Alpha, but a living ancestor continuing to fulfill those more narrow roles he is still suited for.

There are many ways to use this three-type male framework to track individual and group dynamics and to survive as you move from one group setting to another. I think I began using this framework delivering ice cream to supermarkets. I had 34 stops. The names and personalities were many, but the hierarchies had the same players. At a glance I could spot the alpha, the betas and the omega. This is similar to how a ball player reads the players on another team, keeping a sharp eye for the out-of-place piece of the moving puzzle. The ice cream delivery gig will make a good example for another time. For now I will simply explain why I like the three-type view of the masculine axis.

First, we are referring to a relationship to masculine group dynamics that may be partly situational, like the ten generals of Athens, all competing Alpha males, but on the day of battle, only the one whose day it was to lead is recognized as such.

I am most concerned with a man's natural inclination. When I managed a grocery store, I wanted the person to fit the job. In predicting danger and aggression the right personality fit is even more crucial. The three types will each have a wide range of subtypes which only concern me in their extreme specificity, in the form of the actual person.

ALPHA MALES are leaders, have a huge range of ability, and the desire to lead; from the cop who questions himself every time he has to verbally impose his will to the megalomaniac politician who just can't get enough of playing with his human chess pieces. What sets an Alpha apart is that the leadership role itself, the act of compelling others to act in accord with his wishes or the demands of the hierarchy, and the responsibility to do so, does not, in and of itself, repel, stress or diminish him. In our socially-engineered world, where we are taught in sports, work and the military that everyone has what it takes to be a leader and where we are subject to hierarchies that attempt to make us as interchangeable as possible, it is sometimes easy to forget that most people are not cutout for true leadership.

BETA MALES are people who are most comfortable with following a leader, following social trends, abiding by fashion norms and social conventions, following orders, etc. Beta males range from gung ho "Yes, sir, how high sir!" guys to griping job-slackers and hesitant followers. The vast majority of men are Betas. They might be like sheep or like rabid dogs, but what they have in common is that they don't want to be the first to take a risk and do not want to be alone.

OMEGA MALES are alienated men, men apart, men more comfortable operating alone than leading or following. This personality is either vilified, or romanticized as a "lone wolf" type, when it comes to neo-tribalism, which entirely misses the point. This person can range from a hoarder, to a scholar, to a serial killer, or a crack-head hunting cigarette butts in the cracks of the pavement. Many people fail to realize that in many masculine settings, an Alpha will use the Omega to achieve his hierarchal ends and the Omega will serve in this way as a means of maintaining his level of autonomy. The best example of this from myth would be King Arthur [Alpha warrior] and Merlin the Wizard [Omega advisor]. In American history we have the example of an Alpha and Omega working together in the opposite direction with Sitting Bull [Alpha advisor] Crazy Horse [Omega warrior], and in the more usual fashion as Wyatt Earp [Alpha law enforcer] and Doc Holiday [Omega killer]. The movie *Tombstone* actually does an excellent job of sketching the masculine axis across the cast of characters.

A Sludgy Axis

I am tempted to remind myself that the masculine axis is fluid, but it is not.

I am clearly an Omega personality and am probably more alienated than anyone I know. However, I have made a fine Beta when needed. I'm a good team member, good crew member and make things as easy for my boss as possible—so that he won't give me any shit... because when he does, I walk, because I'm really an outcast. Although I have a deep antipathy for leadership positions I have functioned as a coach and even spent four years running a 110 person business. However, as a coach, I defer to my assistant more often than not and lapse into a specialized role. As a general manager I only succeeded because I controlled staffing. I hired and promoted the few leaders I found, while I advised them and trained their people, moderated disputes, hired, rewarded, disciplined and fired all on an individual basis. I never addressed more than two people at a time. I only made this leadership position work according to my loner nature because I was an expert in the business among the ignorant, and in a position to shape the situation. I would never be able to lead men in combat or on a ball field.

I'm happiest doing the job myself, and can tolerate advising and instructing within limits which are generally the roles alienated men fall into, engaging in specialized pursuits apart, and usually for the benefit of the main body.

Imagine the Masculine Axis with the Alphas in the center, surrounded by the Betas, which are orbited by the Omegas. The Omega is really no threat to the leader other than as an assassin in criminal settings. He is a threat to the Betas and hence the Alpha's asset to be had or lost, used or squandered. My theory is skewed toward the alienated person as I composed it for the benefit of men somewhat like myself, seeking a way that did not require them to be a follower or a leader. My reading of Melville's *Typee* and Jack Donovan's work convinced me that what I was articulating was the taboo personality, a probable byproduct of any hierarchy which has functioned long enough to generate human debris.

As to where a Sigma would fit into this aggression-oriented view of masculine interaction, I would like to see that articulated by someone familiar with the full spectrum or personality types that the question suggests.

Pondering on Weathertop

Impressions of J.R.R. Tolkien's *The Fellowship of the Ring*

The reader should be familiar with the movies based on Tolkien's iconic trilogy; if he is not, having read the trilogy twice, this reader found no material contradiction between the movies and the novels they were based upon. The movies are faithful enough to the text and seem to harbor less Hollywood poison than any other film adaptation, that when I feel moved to revisit the story, I choose the expedient of the movie. For this viewing, I sat with a companion who had never seen the movies, nor completed the trilogy, but had read *The Hobbit*.

Her initial thought was to view them according to the story chronology with *The Hobbit* first. However, having viewed all three installments of *The Hobbit*, I informed her that unlike *The Lord of the Rings*, the three-part screen adaptation of *The Hobbit* had progressively demonstrated the onset of the Hollywood cancer. Filmed at a video game pace, *The Hobbit* movies surrendered to the most virulent politically correct tropes: Nordic negroes, a killer heroine flying through the air, slaying armies of armored giants, and a completely inserted subplot involving an interracial love affair between an elf princess who rejects her heritage and a doomed martyr dwarf. By the end of the last movie, I was so disgusted and had developed such a vicious hatred for dwarves and elves that I embarrassed my son by cheering gutturally with a fist of power to every stroke delivered by the only masculine figures fighting for their heritage–the orc chieftains played by modern Maori stunt men. The message of Tolkien's *The Fellowship of the Ring* so keenly preserved in the movie, with orcs representing the evils of industrialism and mass, mongrelized society, was so twisted out of all shape by the same production group a mere ten years later that the only thing left retaining a shred of Tolkien's metaphor was the depiction of the defiant orc chieftain battling against all odds, against the greed of men and elves and dwarves, in a doomed fight to preserve his tribe.

I revisited *The Fellowship of the Ring* from a mythic, masculine perspective, the only passion I have left to me, I find myself identifying with the ring wraiths in this way. I identify the following themes:

1. The inevitable corruptibility of men in power,
2. The innocence and hope of children,
3. The damnation of the elite,
4. The industrialization of life,

5. The primacy of nature,
6. The alchemy of knowledge,
7. Intercession.

We'll come back to these as they appear in the story line.

First, we want to cover some plot elements. The persistent foibles of two of the hobbits, Merry and Pippin, seem to represent the stupidity and utility of common people who exist purely in the temporal sphere, who have no inkling of the transcendent. While the two lesser hobbits get the fellowship in plenty of trouble, demonstrating little or no forethought, their survivability, reflected in their knack for navigating the violence of the physical world, is crucial to the quest. These commoner hobbits both facilitate Frodo's escape from the forces of evil as well as assuring that the evil forces are aware of the quest.

Frodo and Sam represent incorruptibility and honor, elements which rise up enough in the course of human affairs to frustrate the drive toward the dark side. They are, however, shown to be too trusting and direct, and certainly too few to be able to survive without the assistance of baser types of their kind, i.e., Merry and Pippin. Taken together, the four hobbits represent a synergy of the honor, purity, criminality and recklessness necessary to frustrate any systemic effort to eradicate the human spirit. Each pair of hobbits make a whole as well as the two pairs together.

As a general note, Tolkien stands out as a philologist, a folklorist, and a mythologist. His story-telling skills when compared to commercial fiction writers, from contemporaries like Edgar Rice Burroughs down to writers of suspense, like Robert Ludlum and Eric Van Lustbader [creator and inheriting author of the "Bourne" adventure series], are fairly pedestrian. Tolkien could never write a whodunit or a mystery novel. He relies on stupid mistakes, as do authors of modern horror scripts; and relies on improbable resurrections as do authors, of religious texts. Tolkien's genius is in the texture of his world and the composition of its moral fabric.

The sacrifice of Gandalf in the ultimate cause results in the breaking of the fellowship that had been formed toward that same ultimate goal. In order for Tolkien's themes to be played out, the breaking of the fellowship was necessary in terms of the plot, so necessary, that it is indicated in the title, with the different characters, separating but still committed to the same goal, we have a story that evokes the Grail romances in "The Life of Arthur" by Mallory.

Theme One: The Inevitable Corruptibility of Men in Power

The central theme of the trilogy is clearly the ring, as indicated by the Title. The ring of power is a mythic artifact representing the corruption of power or the dictum that power corrupts; absolute power corrupts absolutely. This represents the gravity or the moral weight that affects all of the lesser thematic elements of the story.

Theme Two: The Innocence and Hope of Children

The characters Frodo and Sam represent innocence and hope respectively. As the element of innocence, Frodo supplies resistance to corruption. As the element of Hope, Sam represents the courage and commitment to honor necessary for the persistence of the purity embodied in Frodo. If this were a modern, more concise tale, Frodo and Sam would be the conflicting elements of one character.

Theme Three: The Damnation of the Elite

This is represented by the conference in Rivendell and embodied by the person of Boromir, the son of the steward of the great kingdom of Gondor. Boromir wears the trappings of the hero and when in combat, acts heroically, but he is in fact a representative of the intrinsically corrupt elite class and can barely keep his hands off of the ring for the entirety of the fellowship's quest. As a character, Boromir annoys the viewer every bit as much as the politician annoys the voter, for both the viewer and the voter are compelled to back the representative in his struggle, knowing full well that he will betray the cause. The lady, Galadriel, and Boromir's deep dread of her in the meeting, recall the politicians fleeting realization that he lacks the character of his ancestral counterpart, the hero.

Theme Four: The Industrialization of Life

Saruman, the wizard, Lord of Isengard, represents the industrialist and the modern nation state, his orcs representing the soldier of machine warfare,--the warrior debased to a cipher—nameless and without identity. Saruman's campaign to industrialize his formerly sacred fiefdom was very strongly represented in the film, possibly inspired by Tolkien's experience in World War I.

Theme Five: The Primacy of Nature

This is best illustrated, in Tolkien's hands, by the unnatural ring wraiths, the nine dark riders that oppose the nine members of the fellowship. The wraiths, "were once kings of men," and so they appear the shadowed outline of what once might have been a hero king. These are the corrupt leaders of industrialized mankind. Interestingly, they appear unable to travel except by road, and the members of the fellowship fall into deepest peril at their hands when they gather in a town and when they seek the shelter of the ancient fortress turret now known as

Weathertop, the most powerful and therefore most corrupt, and they only apply their power along the well-trodden axis of man's technological development. This is most tellingly illustrated when they attempt to cross a river with a diminished flow, only to be washed away by a torrent, called down by the elf princess.

Theme Six: The Alchemy of Knowledge

In *The Lord of the Rings,* there are only a handful of wizards. Foremost among these are Gandalf and Saruman. These two characters offer a dualistic study of light and dark sorcery, sorcery being the use of knowledge to affect the course of events, with the character of Saruman representing the corruption of humanity which occurs when knowledge is bent to serve power. Gandalf represents the sacrifice necessary to use knowledge as a means of thwarting the accrual of power in corrupt hands.

Theme Seven: Intercession

The character of Aragorn represents the reluctant hero who fears taking on the powers of kingship from his knowledge that kings, most clearly exemplified by his corruptible ancestor, are often corrupted by their assumption of power. Conversely, Aragorn represents the hope of common people for an intercessor, a supra-elite being who possesses enough power in his office that he is above the corrupting pursuit of power that typifies the twisted souls such as Boromir, and might check that corruptible pursuit. Consider again the scene at Weathertop, where Aragorn, the man who would reluctantly accept kingship, fights off all nine of the undead ring wraiths, who have through their pursuit of power degenerated from his heroic form to a state of empty predation. Aragorn represents to the ring wraiths what they once might have been and so they fear him, just as they represent what he might become, and so he drives them off like figments of a nightmare. This is the scene, midway through the first of the three novels comprising the trilogy, that predicts the third novel and names it, *The Return of the King*.

Taken as a whole, *The Fellowship of the Ring* is a study of the hero in various forms, striving to survive a system contrived to make him an impossibility. In this sense, as long as there is a hero, there's hope.

The Wishing Well

Gender and Race in Horror Movies

I take the horror genre overall as reaching its modern form with Bram Stoker's *Dracula,* just over a hundred years ago. The horror movies seen by my parents' and grandparents' generation held to this same form. The form places a small group of people in the path of some supernatural horror, which in many cases has a sympathetic element as the monstrous threat is often personalized to reflect a more primal human state. Looking at Dracula, he is, in a sense, a super masculine threat to a man and two women. This man and a small group of companions attempt to defend the women. They fail in saving the first woman but succeed in saving the second, although one of their number is killed. There is still an element of the heroic in this character's death, also in the battling against the monstrous, and the sense of heroism is even granted the monster who was battling the entire world.

This last element, the heroic monster, has gained increasing traction with the viewing public as society has increased in size and scale, magnifying the individual's sense of alienation. This got to the point in the early 1980s that monstrous horror became a type of fantasy literature, spawning fantasy movies in which the viewer identifies with protagonists who are themselves monsters, vampires and werewolves predominantly. This is essentially no longer horror but fantasy, as the viewer identifies with unthinkably powerful beings who literally feed on the greater part of humanity which is reduced to a herd.

So what has happened to the horrific element, and how has it been treated in films, particularly those directed at a youthful audience? In fantasy films, we get one element of the moral degradation of the hero by sketching him in the form of the monster which feeds on the people that the traditional hero was supposed to represent and defend. Heroes, as they were primally understood, no longer exist, having been replaced by superheroes. Though it's beyond the scope of this article, this writer believes that the superhero genre was conceived in order to eradicate the idea of the hero, of placing the hero in godlike and monstrous form, where previously heroism was within the reach of every man. In ancient epics, the hero rose from among men to challenge the petty gods and their monsters. Superheroes and superhero villains have very little in common with the ancient hero but are more like the petty gods, with their narrow powers and their monstrous pets.

This leaves us with the modern horror story of the slasher variety, which is entirely bereft of the supernatural and of the heroic, and is reduced to a sadistic hunt. Let us examine the standard tropes in this end time genre:

1. The protagonists are urban/suburban youths.

2. The setting is rural.

3. The killers or the monster are exclusively male.

4. They are always Caucasian men.

5. The protagonists continually act against their own self-interest and survival, which empowers the viewer. The endearing aspect of this genre is that viewers will yell warnings at the stupidly acting protagonist who is about to meet a grim fate.

6. Victims who die early, representing the iniquitous price paid for the bad course charted by the group, traditionally come in three varieties: slut, jock and a person of color.

7. Masculine resistance, initiative and intervention by or on behalf of the victims always clearly fails. A classic example of this, combining tropes 6 and 7, is from the movie, *The Shining* in which the black clairvoyant adult played by Scatman Crothers who is coming to save the boy clairvoyant from the evil white father is immediately butchered upon entering the hotel. Black characters in general are cast as victims, are in the minority, and are killed in a way reflecting the hopeless condition of their kind in general. This has recently changed and will be discussed below.

8. The primary target of the monster is a virtuous white woman [sometimes a precociously moral child], who, crucially is not believed by her husband or male love interest when she realizes she is being hunted.

9. The survivor of such a story is either a child or a young woman who did not have sex during the course of the story.

10. Any hero-type actions that are successful will be committed by this escaping, non-masculine victim of innocence.

The changing point for the status of the lone black victim in these predominantly Caucasian herds of victims was in the unique, heroic horror movie, *Deep Blue*. In this late 1990s movie, an evil female scientist uses a heroic white man as a tool in her breeding of super sharks. When the sharks predictably turn on their makers, the heroics of the man work, and the evil woman is killed by her monster. There is also an endearing scene when the cook in the experimental aquarium, a black character played by LL Cool J is wading through his flooded kitchen and just as the reader expects him to be devoured by a shark, he says to himself something to the effect that he was in a bad spot, because in a movie, this is where the black guy always gets killed. At this point the story diverts from the standard horror narrative and could be classified as a type of heroic science fiction. Another notable example of this type of heroic science fiction with many heroic masculine elements, made in the same period in the early 2000s is *Pitch Black*, which become the starting point for a cycle about a primally masculine hero struggling against an evil system.

The movies discussed above with the science fiction angle and a heroic element might be seen as reactionary films, just as the slasher genre typified by the *Halloween* and *Friday the Thirteenth* series had become impotent to the point where the audiences were cheering on the villain. Since that time, there has been a serious effort to remake some of these films based on more realistic understanding of psychopathic killers with more sympathetic victims and more well-rounded monstrous white men. To bring us up to date, I'd like to discuss two movies that I recently watched, which are targeted to a youthful audience in such a way as to maximize appeal among white female and black viewers.

Hush is a film about a deaf woman who writes novels alone in a prodigiously windowed cottage in the middle of the woods. She is estranged from the big city and her black ex-boyfriend, a distant hunk who remains improbably supportive of her writing career. She and her neighbors, a traditional couple, attractive woman and very masculine, handsome white man, come under attack by a white male psychopath. This pretty much tells you all you need to know about the movie. The he-man, next door neighbor, will be butchered by the geek with the knife, who is hunting the women, and the primary female victim becomes a gritty heroine slaying her hunter, with the underlying moral of the story being that she should not have left her black boyfriend in the city. The movie ends with police cars coming out of the city to save her: rural bad, city good; white man bad, black man good.

The next movie, *The Watcher,* features the only type of married couple that Hollywood wants to promote these days, a white woman and a black man, who move into a house that appears to be haunted. The previous owners of the house were an elderly Asian couple, victimized by the ghost. The real estate agent who heartlessly sold the haunted house is a white woman. The creepy neighbors consist of a nosy white woman and her retarded teenage son. The good neighbors are black: a well-heeled, strong woman with a husband who is a Hollywood stunt man. The entire police department consists of females and black men. There is not an adult Caucasian male in the movie. Unlike the ineffectual Caucasian man of the traditional slasher flick, the black men believe the woman is under threat and are able to defeat the evil that threatens the white wife. Up until the final scene, they think that this evil is the nosy white woman next door. But in the final scene, just after they adopt the poor retarded son of the nosy white woman, it is revealed that he is the psychopathic killer and terrorizer of women–suddenly shedding his boyish handicap and turning into a towering monster of a man. The moral of the story is that white people are either crazy or evil. That's it.

To review, the horror genre, with few exceptions, horror from the age of silent film in the 1920s and up through the early 1960s was infused with heroic elements, generally placing a virtuous woman in danger. Danger she cannot defeat on her own.

Ignoring the branching fantasy genre typified by romanticizing the monster, essentially founded by *Interview with a Vampire* by Anne Rice, and the branching into science fiction horror tales, beginning with *Aliens* [featuring a strong female protagonist, but also masculine heroism], remaining horror has tended to the gross slasher flicks discussed above and of more mature supernatural horror stories which follow the satanic threat complex, which eradicates heroism without targeting rural white men as the ultimate evil.

Overall, since the cultural revolution of the 1960s, horror films in general have stridently attacked the notion of heroic action as impossible and even childish.

Secondarily, since the 1960s, villains in non-supernatural horror have all been rural white men. Even the location of many supernatural horror tales ends up being rural.

The tertiary message of horror films, that the man will not support the woman in times of crisis, seems to be the solid third runner, until very recently, with the reintroduction of heroics in the form of the female victim and her black man, who is properly submissive to the fears of his white wife, rather than dismissive. The addition of these last themes strike one as overly contrived and may ultimately occupy a passing fad or niche in the genre. Will these themes of black masculine virtue expand, resurrecting the dead hero in limited guise?

What is of most interest to this viewer is the obliteration of the idea of the hero, especially when taken together with the civic neo-paganism of the wildly popular superhero genre.

But returning to the horror genre itself, of that narrow classification of film that focuses solely on the horrific actions of men, heroism might be viewed as a necessary casualty in the process of scaring the viewer in his/her seat. For the introduction of a single competent man with a handgun would shatter the fragile story line, built as it is on bad decisions.

What then, is the main thrust of slasher-variety horror fiction?

It is quite obviously the same theme that one sees in such iconic films as *Deliverance, Forest Gump, The Green Mile,* in the Denzel Washington films, *Man on Fire, Safe House,* and *The Equalizer,* in the little known 70s film, *Southern Comfort,* in the classic and remake versions of *The Hills Have Eyes, Texas Chainsaw Massacre,* and *Halloween* movies and in the entire crop of recent Rob Zombie films such as *The Devil's Rejects,* and even in the quirky *Secret Window,* that white men are evil, an incredibly lethal strain of humanity. However, taking the broad overview, it is obvious that the most evil white man is the rural one, who owns a gun and lives in hills or words. Failing that he's an Eastern European white man.

[Since the late 1980s, action films have featured Eastern European bad guys in profusion. In a recent viewing of an FBI action TV show called *Numbers,* in five episodes there was not a single person of color or female among the swarming army of white male villains, though black heroes did fight alongside conflicted white agents against them. Police dramas are not generally set in rural locales, but feature an overwhelming preponderance of white male criminals, in the very urban settings that are in fact dominated by criminals of color.]

The connection between evil, the white man and the rural setting is so strong in the horror genre, that its premier author Stephen King [advertisements for King's books and stories about his work dominate and literally keep afloat no less than two horror magazines] has penned two novels about a white male writer seeking solitude in the remote countryside, with this isolation from the city turning him into a vehicle for evil, in both cases attacking his own family.

Upon consideration of the cinematic weight—even in comedy with films such as *City Slickers*—that equates rural white men with evil, and realizing that all of the filmmakers and actors involved are suburban or urban persons, we see a vast prejudice. For everyone in America knows that all of the most violent and deadly environments are cities and their sprawling suburbs, in which the vast majority of violence is committed by people of color. Yet films across a variety of genres depict urban environments as safe havens, people of color as so virtuous and non-violent as to render these characters uninteresting, and depict rural white men as prodigious killers, with the rural enclaves, that in actual fact see almost no murder, appearing in movies as virtual slaughter zones for trophy killing.

Could it be that somewhere deep in the elite, urban American soul, there remains a cultural memory that when the white slaves brought to this country in chains to work plantations[1] that are now paved over by urban centers, that they escaped the slave matrix through either flight, hard work or insurrection and fled, gun in hand, to those very hills and forests that modern filmmakers have peopled with monsters for over a half century? Is the modern slasher flick nothing more than a retelling of the tale the slave master of old told his white and black slaves, that to leave the plantation was to cast off the fetters of security for the perils of the savage wilderness, peopled by predatory outcasts?

---

[1] A plantation planted people to form a taxation and labor base for claiming possession in the name of the home country.

Ishmael and The Pale Usher

'Would You Have Been Different If You Had Grown Up in a More Decent Setting than Baltimore?' A Man Question from Sean

The answer that came directly to my mind was, Ishmael, "I would have ended up being like Ishmael, the same outsider personality, but stuck in a machine barely human enough to accommodate my conscience."

Last year, almost exactly 11 months ago, when I met Ishmael in the Salt Lake City airport, it was like meeting a twin from whom I had been separated at birth. I've met some folks like that through my writing—Nero the Pict being another—but no one else who I immediately sensed so alike in terms of outlook and other-look.

Ishmael and I were each luckier than the other in some ways and physically different enough for our material aspect to make a big difference in how the world looked upon us. My world is far more twisted than his and seems to have twisted me more. However, with the realization among many of us outliers that the greater world of postmodern civilization is based on a lie filled foundation, reflected in the immediate ostracism and even criminalization of truthful speech—such as the notion that our leaders raping children for sport is not to be discussed–seems to place the moral superstructure of our devolved spiritual world more in line with the evil that is Baltimore and places like it than the Rocky Mountains and its people.

As the evil of the sickening world reaches its vile claws to clutch at Ishmael's mountain, he has reached out for news of his future, for insights into what it is like to live where Wrong has won, where Right and Might are by definition separate and the very words we breathe are heard through fiendishly twisted baffles, where hate is the sacred song of innocent martyrdom and truth is regarded as evil, declared the very screeching of the demonic pit.

The world has shaped us in different ways, but I know we are the same.

Toward a vision of this end, I have worked for some years on a book that languishes on my desk in its final stages, The Pale Usher, an interpretation of the extended introduction to Moby Dick, those first 30 odd chapters in which the protagonist, Ishmael, separates from society by stages, largely with the help of a savage raised in the heathen parts of the world, a man who is clearly his mythic twin. I began this book six months before Ishmael contacted me by email, but continued it largely thanks to his encouragement, and will take off posting a day this week to complete it and have it shipped out to the roof of our expanded world, ahead of my outward flight from Harm City a month from now.

A Man

Robert E. Howard on Masculine Racial Consciousness

"The kisses and love-cries of women fade and pall, but the sword sings a fresh song with each stroke."

-Robert E. Howard, *Marchers of Valhalla,* Asgrimm

"A man is no better and no worse than his feelings regarding the women of his blood, which is the true and only test of racial consciousness. A man will take to himself the stranger woman, and sit down at meat with the stranger man, and feel no twinges of race-consciousness. It is only when he sees the alien man in possession of, or intent upon, a woman of his blood, that he realizes the difference in race and strain."

-Robert E. Howard, *Marchers of Valhalla,* Hialmar

Throughout Howard's works, his Aryan heroes cross racial boundaries, becoming blood-brothers with alien tribesmen, lovers of strange—even extra-human—

women, some saving good black folk from their savage oppressors, others delving insanely deeply into tribal hatreds and blood feuds with their racial cousins. But through all of their brutal adventures they do not let go of their identity, for just as there is no such creature as a superhero, erasing the trials of the true hero in effigy to appease the postmodern worm on his couch of sloth, there is no such thing as a human hero without racial identity, tribal loyalty, and most of all, other men, heroes of rival ethnicities ready and willing to pour their wrath upon him.

Marchers of Valhalla and the other stories collected in that volume reveal the ideal of the hero and the nature of the waters tapped by the storyteller dipping into the heroic well of souls—it is blood, the ancestral link that binds and defines, that substance that is the subterranean river of heroes that is mankind's only hope when all of our petty artifice fails in the face of the bloodless, soulless, monstrous.

Our Ancestors

Ishmael and James Discuss Their Forefathers

James, I sat and pondered for a while after reading the article below. Mixing the races has occurred here between Mexicans, Whites, Native Americans, the latter being who really are natives. We have been moving as a people for all our history. My cousins from the south were dark-skinned, black hair, Cherokee. My other cousins were red, and blonde, brown-headed. We noticed but it was never mentioned in hostile terms. We got along very well. In fact, I fought with the redhairs the most. We were proud of our ancestors, all of them. What is your view of your past families?

-Ishmael

https://www.lewrockwell.com/2017/03/fred-reed/social-justice-warriors-bubonic-plague/

Masculine Axis

Ishmael, I come from four stocks that I know of, from most recent to most ancient in terms of their coming to North America. I am superstitious concerning my ancestry and have lately begun paying more attention to how I feel when I consider the bloodlines that converge in me.

Most recent are the Germans, named Kern, who came in the 1870s to start up a pudding business. They were Catholics leaving a Protestant land for Catholic Maryland. I do not feel any great attachment to this quarter of my family, being half of my mother's money-grubbing people. The Kerns were very strict and would use physical punishment, but only as a backup form of discipline, not the default.

This is the secondary aspect of my maternal line, strong and patriarchal.

The stern, acquisitive kraut in me is weak—a feeling of distance, seems to separate me from that branch, despite my admiration of the men I have learned from.

In 1901 came the English Roys, who were child orphans sold to French Canadians by the British government circa 1800. My beloved and wise grandmother Alberta LaFond, who beat cancer for 50 years and was very intelligent, forever fiercely hated the British for doing this to her ancestors. She told me stories about Elzear Roy. I identify strongly with this quarter of my family, who are artistic and bookish. Elzear was an herbalist and shipwright, whose best friend was an Indian named, Mister Short Step. The Roys never struck their children.

This is the dominant aspect of my paternal line.

The English orphan in me is strong, idea-oriented and angry.

The French LaFond family, which Alberta Roy married into, were kind, artistic folk, many of whom settled in Fall River, Mass. Alberta came south from Canada as an infant of six months and married into the LaFond family there. The main branch of the LaFond family is more physical and is found mostly in the upper Mississippi basin in the U.S. I fought one of these lugs once, and he was made of much stronger stuff than I. The LaFonds were, I think, an older New World family than the Roys, but I do not know.

The LaFond quarter of my family is the biggest mystery to me as my grandfather died when I was six. He was a sign painter, a very kindly man who called Alberta "Roy," with a tender affection. He was not a physically strong man like the Kerns or Quaids of my maternal side.

This is the secondary aspect of my paternal line.

The LaFonds did not strike their children and I blindly but ardently feel my association with them like a haze sunk over my dream.

The Irish Quaids, originally McQuaids, came to Maryland in the mid-1600s as Irish Catholic servants of the Anglo-Irish leaders of the colony. I think they settled in southern Maryland, engaged in servant-overseeing—good slaves that they were—did well and made their way to Baltimore Town and never left that accursed pit of their servitude. There was a smiling roughness to the Quaids which I never liked but which I inherited. My one Uncle Joe was a big, kind man. His five sisters had nice figures and married exceptional men whom I learned a lot from.

This is the primary aspect of my maternal line, a family that moved genetically rather than geographically from its obediently frustrated Irish roots.

The Quaids beat their children and although I resent their lineage, I have a lingering sense of attachment that pervades my dream-life and is most frustratingly apparent in my irrational attachment to this damned place. I can literally feel my way around Baltimore—have always been able to, and even as a small boy of six, felt the pull of places near but beyond my range—and have never been physically lost in this accursed place.

Relating this was a strange experience, Ishmael.

Thanks

Our Forefathers

Confessions of a Reluctant Baby Boomer

Our forefathers built this city that we fled, let burn, let decay.

Our forefathers were born in the lean times and brought us into the fattest age man has been born to and we smoked dope, popped pills, snorted coke, shot heroin, smoked crack—and it's gone, the greatest treasure chest left to a generation looted for a party.

Our forefathers fought the greatest war in history and emerged the sole victors, while we send robots to bomb our medieval enemies.

Our forefathers escaped the mighty Earth to tread the ghostly moon. Not only did we fail to follow in their footsteps we betrayed our sons by dismantling Our Kind's single greatest achievement.

Our forefathers we mocked, our sons betrayed. We cannot be punished with guilt, for we are, in our abysmal ignorance, blind to our crimes.

There is only one pit big enough to contain our moral stench: Eternity, gaping wide.

Whiteman

Who Are You?

I prefer White Devil, Neanderthal, Yeti, Caveman, Polar Bear and especially Paleface, to being a mere-near negated white man. But if white man I must be, I elect to be a Whiteman.

In the face of our systematic negation, of the top down erasure of our culture, our identity, our masculinity–of our very souls–some have been pushed into or retreated into identity politics, often as a result of negative identity politics, of our vilification for the crime of our birth pigmentation, of our homo-zoological designation.

Currently, the worst thing a person can be, is a Caucasian Man–the face of evil in our sock puppet age. Being a white man–a color that I have only seen on a freak who treated himself with bleach–is evil in the new mono-cultural collective. Many of us who failed to deny our race and gender role at the crucial moment have been labeled white and pushed into that cultural kill box and hence fight from there. I propose, however, not to resist from the single gross interior line assigned us by these enemies who framed the conflict, but to operate out of a more organic and resistant framework of interior cultural lines.

The most compromised men in the current social order are identified as black, yet they are not black, but mixed race people, ranging from predominantly African to predominantly European in ancestry. If you, like the black man, have been falsely labeled with the overly-generalized and crucially belligerent category of white [really, the absence of color and not applicable to humans in a clear-thinking sense] I suggest rebelling. If you are a black man, I suggest rebelling and allying with some clear-thinking person of another race.

Our macro-racial worldview is essentially zoological, not ethnic. This comes from the Universalist idea of Christendom, of being a Christian in a heathen world, which was extra-ethnic, but at least spiritual. This was overtaken by the British mercantilist notion of the Whiteman, which was a way to get related racial groups to support British claims in colored nations and took on a meta-zoological tone with the grouping of humans in five vast racial groups. This was a form of racial negation, a way of honor-binding the Irishman, the Welshman, the Scotsman, the Cornishman, the Englishman, to the false notion of the British-man, which, interestingly gets redlined by this Word program I am writing in when I try to make a single word of it...

When old style authors, like Robert E. Howard, wrote of race–when Homer wrote of a people they referred to tribes and confederacies. With the dehumanizing zoological reduction of humanity to herds of variously colored cattle, our masters–invisible economic gods, veiled Oz-like characters and hook-nosed caricatures, have a means of ethnic negation, a way by which we might be packaged, boxed, shipped and sold according to their political needs.

Gone forever is the notion of being an Irishman, a Dark-Irish, a Kern, a clansman, perhaps allied with other Gaels in the face of Anglos, perhaps allied with Anglos in the face of a mongrel horde, but distinct.

Now we are just, what, white men?

The absence of color?

No, we are men, men have kin, kin form clans and tribes and we are distinct–not cattle, not chattel, not fucking beans to be sorted and counted in a global warehouse, sorted in buckets rather than slots for the ease of some puppet-master, but men, men with a tribe, men who build societies, who form honor-threads, who push their blood and ideas downstream through the filthy sewer of managerial politics in search of what we were and may once again be.

Don't be a black man, be hotep, a Yaruba man, an Ebo man, a Ghanaboy, be anything but the absence of light, which is what your designation means in plain language.

Masculine Axis

Don't be a white man, be a Southern Man, be an Appalachian Man, be a Rocky Mountain Man, be an Irishman, a Scotsman, hell, be a goddamned Englishman, if need be, be anything but the absence of color.

And if need be, when you find yourself alone, the last Gael in some asphalt lot paved for your extinction, at least leave a ghost trace and take one of those bastards with you.

Don't think they aren't coming for us once we've all been negated into our broadest commonality or alienated into our narrowest eccentricity.

They're coming and the last thing they want to face in the extinguishing moment of their self-erased haunting of this meat-puppet matrix is a MAN with an IDENTITY.

Send them to their version of secular Hell–paint the empty sky of this consumption matrix with their screaming, skid-mark shade and at least you've died with what they never had, a SOUL.

Emasculation Nation

A Country Girl Gets a Mangina Wakeup Call

The author's niece apologizes for doubting his estrogenic prophecy.

I never was 100% sure what you meant by men becoming so feminine, but now I understand.

I'm sorry I doubted you.

Well, there wasn't that much to it. There was just some fat balding guy at work who whined for a ridiculous amount of time about his computer in a different spot, the desk hadn't been tidied up, he didn't like the mouse, etc. He couldn't even call tech support by himself. The office is mostly women, so I hear that kind of complaining all day, but it was the strangest thing to hear it from a man. I try my best not to have double standards, but I totally failed this time.

Masculine Axis

She succeeded in being a woman and has therefore failed the artificial standards imposed upon her perceptions. Men are at their best when women expect them to uphold a masculine standard.

Unmanly Managers

'With the drop in male testosterone, is this hormonal or evolution?'

Ishmael writes:

James, your advice or criticism is always welcome, the salary for upper management was 1.5 to maybe 2 times more than the foremen, the operators made about 10 to 15 percent less than the foremen, depending on experience, hard work was a plus, now the upper crust make 3 to 4 times what a good operator makes, I noticed the disparity grew after the snowflake-minded replaced the old guard. I think this is a good example of one reason why we have the current problems in the workplace, they cry about equality for minorities, but shit on the blue collar white guys, they are not lazy men, most come from rural backgrounds, the operators are good men deserve more for their efforts.

Why do the weak-ass manginas dislike the operators? The operators do all the dirty hard jobs that keep this place in business, this was an area that caused me grief as a manager. They think, because of their position, that hard work is for chumps, I butted heads with them, why I refused anymore advancement.

We do not operate on taxes. We get our income from providing services to 6,000 customers. But this has turned into another racket, remind me to explain the workings of this fucked up system of rabbit warrens, I'm just one of the old guard.

To add, I would rather work with Varg and LaFond in hell than kiss the ass of the system, my hypocrisy only goes so far!

Ishmael, your question was, "Why do the weak-ass manginas dislike the operators? The operators do all the dirty hard jobs that keep this place in business."

Observe, that for my answer, I simply copied and pasted the qualifying context that was the second sentence, "The operators do all the dirty hard jobs that keep this place in business."

The master-slave mindset and its politics of hierarchical envy that dominate the American mentality ensures that the management class, people who are essentially impotent and useless outside of the rung in the power structure they occupy, have an inherent jealousy for the working man, just as bull dykes have penis envy. Management is a parasitic process as envisioned in American Culture by its proponents. I and the couple other highly effective grocery store managers I have known, all worked alongside our people for numerous reasons, not least of which is morale. We were all castigated by the owners and CEOs. This is a religion to them and makes no logical sense. When I stocked displays in the front of the store, I served a security purpose, a customer service role, a supervisory role, used the activity for instructing clerks and upped the weekly gross by $17K. However, the owners insisted that if I would just sit behind a computer instead of thinking, planning, guarding, supervising and literally pushing dollars through the register on my feet, that I would discover cost cutting and volume increasing secrets hitherto unknown to retail food. They told me this although they and every Baltimore area CEO had failed in this exact pursuit. Every supermarket chain has failed or sold due in part to the inherent uselessness of a Wall Street mentality in a dynamic inventory control situation. Yet there is no move to adopt functional management doctrine. The logical course would have been having me train other store managers on my program and increase volume by millions while improving all management HR, security and customer service roles.

This hatred is an article of faith, Ishmael.

Management hates the working man for the same reason atheists hate Christians, the jealousy of a believer vested in a value system that does not work for those adherents to ancient ways which have always worked for their believers.

Ishmael writes:

James, we have spoken before, and frequently, about the mangina men who seem to hold management positions. Is this, in your opinion a hormonal condition caused by chemicals, PET bottles, factory farm milk, etc., or an evolutionary adaptation to our civilization?

-Ishmael

http://thoughtcatalog.com/jim-goad/2017/03/the-man-who-woke-up-one-morning-with-a-vagina-in-his-forehead/

Ishmael, I'm six books deep nibbling at this question.

There is no doubt that there are some testosterone reducing chemicals out there.

I believe this is at the core of Robert E. Howard's civilization versus barbarism concept. This reduction in masculinity seems to have been cyclic throughout history, with Greeks going from he-men of Homer to the baby sitters of the Romans, the Romans degenerating from the apex man-butchers of the Ancient world to simpering priests fornicating in a decayed Italy, the Germans going from Beowulf to inviting Muslims to rape their daughters, and the Norse going from Wulfere the Skull Cleaver to the bitch boys of a degenerate Europe.

The key seems to be environmental expectations, or the approval matrix of a culture. A while back I cited

Lionel Tiger's book in which he cites a study that showed testosterone scaling wildly different between raw recruits entering Marine Corps boot camp—where they are metaphorically emasculated, like Samson after bedding Delilah via the jar head shave—and then come out of boot camp as relative he-men.

The deep meaning assigned to masculine ritual in tribal societies is universal and the more extreme the ritual, the more those societies wax great, and the more total their success, the more quickly the easy conditions that their conquering fathers made for them results in their degeneration.

Ishmael, put me in front of a typewriter and lay a fine young babe in my bed and I'll keep typing. Seriously, I've done it, have heard, "Are you gay, Mister Jimmy, or are you dead?"

But put me in front of a rugged young guy in the ring and when I step out from between the ropes, his grandmother's virtue won't be safe around me.

I have felt the surge and wane of my own testosterone to be far more extreme in terms of situation than it is according to the chemistry of aging. I am more masculine at 54 than I was at 24, because at age 24, I was trying to fit into a corporate structure in a female dominated workplace.

It is, I think, a cyclic evolutionary adaptation and the reason why current world corporate leadership is focused on universal emasculation and the multisexual transgender agenda—to engineer men out of existence.

You must read *Houston, Houston, Do You Read?* by Alice B. Sheldon.

Imagine you, Shayne and me as astronauts, coming back to an earth with no men 1,000 years from now?

The Four Masculine States

Discussing Nassim Taleb's Work on Human Domestication with Lynn Lockhart

James,

I have been thinking about the Russian soccer hooligan video and also reading *Antifragile*, by Nassim Taleb and trying to connect some ideas. Without getting into the details of the book, the topic of risk taking is important, and I am not sure you have addressed it in terms of civilization, combat arts, or masculinity. The spectrum of risk taking goes from the pathologically timid, he who fears losing his possessions or injuring his body, across to the reckless, who can't judge the risk or doesn't care. There is also the aspect of gambling, what I would consider as playing games of pure chance, like slot machines or lottery tickets. These are risks with no real investment. I have shared with you a piece of his, *How to Legally Own Another Person*, on domestication, or employment as slavery and would love to hear your thoughts.

I will include some choice quotes to entice you to read it:

> Someone who has been employed for a while is giving you the evidence of submission.
>
> ...
>
> Evidence of submission is displayed by having gone through years of the ritual of depriving himself of his personal freedom for nine hours every day, punctual arrival at an office, denying himself his own schedule, and not having beaten up anyone. You have an obedient, housebroken dog.
>
> ...
>
> The best slave is someone you overpay and who know it, terrified of losing his status.
>
> ...
>
> Risk takers can be socially unpredictable people. Freedom is always associated with risk taking, whether it led to it or came from it. You take risks, you feel part of history. And risk takers take risks because it is in their nature to be wild animals.
>
> ...
>
> So while cursing and bad language can be a sign of dog-like status and total ignorance –the "canaille" which etymologically relates these people to dogs; ironically the highest status, that of free-man, is usually indicated by voluntarily adopting the mores of the lowest class.
>
> ...
>
> Watching Putin against others made me realize that domesticated (and sterilized) animals don't stand a chance against a wild predator. Not a single one. Fughedabout military capabilities: it is the trigger that counts.

James writes:

This article, Lynn, was extensive and excellent. It is, however, written from an emasculated and materialistic perspective, the two states being very much conjoined in Western Modernity's witch's brew of unmanning norms. Taleb does not differentiate between genders, admitting that, in the white collar corporate environment he speaks of, these domesticated and "wild" behaviors cross over the gender line and they do. He probably sees the corporate environment as intrinsically male, according to our false modernist convention, which I do not. Perhaps this is illuminated in his book. Corporate environments are "neuter spaces" defeminizing women and unmanning men.

The imitation of the lower class by the upper is as old as Rome, probably older and signals a society in decline. Societies in decline have always—as far as I have been able to determine—suffered in the masculine sphere. This is simple to track within monarchies as succeeding generations of kings and emperors becoming increasingly effeminate, with a reactionary phase of ultra-masculine revival often signaling a last gasp of the culture.

I will focus on this item and the discussion on swearing in the work place as a wild expression of rebellion and reversal to a wild animal state rather than a domesticated state.

Cursing as Wild Devolutionary Rebellion

Taleb deals with two states, wild and domesticated, just as violence analysts traditionally dealt with two states of aggression response, Fight or Flight. These are both over simplified. Aggression response includes Fight, Flight, Posturing and Submission.

Let us apply these four aspects of aggression to the corporate work place, which is a system of aggression against the individual. Fighting gets you fired, flight gets you to the same place, posturing is demonstrated by misbehaving in the work place as Taleb describes and submission keeps you employed or employable.

In terms of emasculation, cursing is a symptom, not a cure. Who traditionally curses the most?

First, sailors, who are the least free and most enslaved military men on the bottom rung, with most sailors of the period in which their swearing was made famous being kidnapping victims or convicts.

The second most famous group of swear mouths is convicts, another frustrated, powerless lot.

The third most foul-mouthed group is black Americans, traditionally at the bottom of American society, bypassed by other ethnicities that have come in beneath them and displaying intergenerational embitterment toward the greater society.

As a person working at the bottom of the economy for 30-plus years, I can tell you that women swear more in the workplace than men of the same class. This makes all the sense in the world when one realizes that the famously foul-mouthed black man is raised, not by a man, but by a woman, who typically displays immense levels of cursing, far beyond any sailor of yore. This behavior is common among women who are forced by circumstance—and this circumstance might be caused by her decision to take government money in exchange for not living with the father of her children—to take on a male role. I can tell you from coaching experience that mothers of athletes are louder and more foul-mouthed than fathers. Cursing is the classic form of powerless, impotent rebellion, blaspheming the social norms that one is unable to overcome or succeed within.

Cursing in the work place is not a sign of wildness but of a feral state, with hallmarks of feminine verbosity rooted in the functional chatter of a gathering social animal who must be keyed to raise the alarm and "chimp out" so that the men might come to their aid.

This point will be better understood if we progress to the four masculine states.

The Four Masculine States

Wild: Typified by neglected children and male children raised by animals, or by a castoff feral human bereft of tribal affiliation, some homeless men fit this rare "Tarzanesque" example, in fiction and myth often represented by the monstrous being, existing at the level of the animals below that of primitive man.

Primal: Disciplined adaptation in the form of learned behavior necessary to prevail over more powerful wild creatures and survive the awesome powers of nature, which, among all Stone Age hunting peoples studied to date, is typified by high functioning silence in the hunting of enemy men and animals and by ritualized noise [music] most often practiced in the presence of women, whereby women gain the impression of men as noisy and hence imitate men's more verbose, at-home ritual rather than their functional field behavior.

Domesticated: Civilized, feminized to varying and usually progressive degrees, until the crucial modern phase when the female too begins to suffer neutering effects.

Feral: Criminal, corrupted, often ultra-masculine in a narrow sense and unbalanced behaviors, typified by a mix of wild, primal and domesticated traits.

Using Taleb's example of Putin and your question of the Russian soccer hooligans who made such work of normal soccer hooligans, we must understand that the normal human is the domesticated one, the soccer hooligan is feral and the Russian Soccer hooligan is self-made and society formed, representing the resurrected Primal practice of training as a unit. Understanding Taleb's wolf example to be on the mark, one must admit that wolves have a primal culture, a society designed around hunting. This is why they worked well with men and have been venerated in primal cults since the beginning. A battle between drunken British soccer hooligans and trained Russian soccer hooligans is like a battle between a pack of feral dogs and a wolf pack—a rout.

Yes, compared to a Western politician Putin is as a wolf to a lap dog.

Let's put Putin on a human scale of wildness and domestication.

Homeless, retarded man =Wild dog
Putin = Wolf
Politician = lap dog
Criminal = feral dog

If we have a single elimination tournament which canine wins?

The lap dog is eaten by the feral dog.

The wolf, being shaped into a paragon of wild canine virtues by the pack system [the canine tribe] gets the best of his undisciplined wilder foe.

The wolf and the feral dog is another wipeout as the feral dog is an imitator, a creature beginning an evolution back to wolf kind, pitted against a fully evolved canine predator.

This little worksheet shows Putin's Russia for what it is, a conscious attempt to rebuild manhood and masculine culture.

Looking at American society via this model we can expand the canine metaphor from lap dog politician to law officer as sheep dog guarding the flock, the prize-fighter as pit bull, soldiers as German shepherds, Doberman pinschers, Irish wolfhounds and other big breeds used in military action in the past and today, with most Americans typing as some kind of house dog.

Lynn, there is a reason why ancient warriors around the world venerated the wolf, why Robert E. Howard constantly used the wolf as the totemic spirit of the tribal man, why the Wolves of Vinland, founded by neo-masculinity advocates in America have taken the wolf as their symbol. To be accurate, we must admit that the wolf pack is a canine tribal structure with values and shared goals and has evolved far beyond the grizzly bear, another canine that gets along on its own due to immense powers, or the skulking jackal, who remains forever marginalized, the animal that Howard used as the totemic image of the cowardly criminal and that in our time is used to describe CIA hit men.

Lynn writes:
James, I like how far you took the dog/wolf analysis. Canines are like our shadows along the path from Wild and Primal to Domesticated and back around to Feral.

I have also observed that women in the workplace curse more than men, though the foulest mouthed person I knew in my short career in finance was a scouser (native of Liverpool) and probably wished he had been a football hooligan in his early days.

Taleb is fun to read. He knows a lot of history and has made some highly original observations. Perhaps we can come back to some of his other writings.

Considering a Primal Human Perspective

A Prequel to the Author's Interview with Lynn Lockhart

Lynn, you've asked me some pretty big questions and also to match wits with a man that has put forth some daunting ideas. Before answering I should make plain my divergence from modern society so that an understanding can occur.

Modernity places man in his masses under ideologies, according to numbers.

I disagree.

Most blatantly I disagree with this approach to violence studies. For instance, the FBI did a comparative analysis of Cocaine-Boom Miami circa 1980 and Dodge City, a century earlier, and declared parity between the two, as they used the number of people under threat, rather than the area of habitat under threat, to determine risk of violence, with their stupid how many deaths in 100,000 equation.

What this showed was that Dodge City and Scarface Miami were both equally violent to an unacceptable degree. Ever since people have used the euphemism that if guns are not taken away from Americans, then our cities will become like "The Wild West"

Well if Baltimore was like the Wild West, we would have had only one homicide last year. That's right, in the year Dodge City was compared to Miami during the drug cartel high tide, one man was killed and he in a voluntary duel over a woman?

Not one murder, just a manslaughter. And, according to the FBI, that is equivalent to Cuban thugs and Columbian narcos hosing down strip malls with machine guns while women and children are shopping?

Why would these geniuses—and they are geniuses, unlike myself, who could not pass the FBI entrance exam—come up with such a false model?

It is simple, the FBI is a branch of the U.S. government, and that government like all other modern state systems is engaged in people farming. Just as shepherds and ranchers count their livestock, so do our handlers.

This, I see as a departure from most of human history and prehistory and has its roots in the two great submissive faiths, Christianity and Islam. Islam means submission, with Muslim men taking names that proudly declare themselves the slaves and servants of God. In Leviticus—in the very book of the

Old Testament that justifies enslavement, God's Chosen People are declared to be his slaves, and should therefore strive to keep one another free of lesser bonds of servitude to outsiders. Being raised Catholic, the idea that I was supposed to submit as a first response to an invocation of authority over my person and my soul was explicit in the ritual kneeling, the constant reference to God, His Son and Prophets "shepherding" their "flock," coupled with the "render unto Caesar what is Caesar's admonition that our parish priests quoted often, indicating that I should be a submissive subject of a government, that I should be livestock.

This doctrine of submission to God and his representatives ensured that Christianity and Islam would be the dominant faiths over most of the planet. And breadth means something here. For these faiths are the blueprints for interacting with the human habitat. There may have been more Hindus at one point, but the adherents to that religion were geographically limited, meaning that fewer aspects of creation fell under their religion's influence. And to minds formed before the materialistic ethos and atheism supplanted so much of the metaphysical construct humanity lives within, Creation meant something, something more than a pile of rock to be rendered into ore and smelted into precious commodities.

Many current critics of the "Abrahamic" faiths take issue with their ethnic or environmental origin. But the fact is that most tribal conquests resulting in civilizations feature violent, herding people displacing the ruling class of a submissive toiling people, who are naturally viewed as cattle, and hence chattel. This was obvious to all pre-modern societies. But modern society operates under a fiction far less plausible than the idea of God, that is the idea of "civil service" or "democracy," the insane notion that the cattle rule the ranch through their bellowing.

Before we continue with the dialogue on Taleb's work, I'd like to make it plain that I see the human being in terms of his relationship to God, which includes the environment, and excludes the herd, the human shepherds. It is obvious that the sacred creeds of submission informed those who structured modern state systems and political ideologies, and that these notions of Dar al-Islam and Christendom contained a more ancient notion of habitable space, not simply the numbers of their flocks.

Before the Industrial Age, Europeans thought in terms of faith far more than race and would speak of "Christian lands," placing people in their living context and beyond it, rather than in our atomized way. Muslims had a similar view and retain far more of it than we secularized Christians.

"…he regarded himself as a citizen, not of a country called Morocco, but of the Dar al-Islam, to whose universalist spiritual, moral and social values he was loyal above any other allegiance."

-Ross E. Dunn on Ibn Battuta

Early Christianity retained much of the ancient, holistic, human worldview, before it was gradually reduced to an ethos to support Modernity. Many Christians [I'm not one] have a sense for this and are continually reinventing the Church on a smaller scale, whether localized or inward-reaching, even bordering on the shamanic, like John Eldredge's *Wild at Heart*, in which he discusses "the silence of fathers" in our denatured society. In a larger sense the ethical systems derived from these religions are, too, silent, which is why I wanted to discuss Taleb's antifragile concept and his related opinion concerning the absence of sacrifice, after this attempt to place it in a truer context.

I'll address Antifragile, and then sacrifice, below.

Thanks for the demanding line of inquiry.

On Becoming Antifragile

The Second Installment of James' and Lynn's Discussion of Nassim Taleb's Antifragile Concept

James,

We have discussed offline Nassim Taleb's concept of antifragility, detailed in his book *Antifragile*. Briefly the concept is that things may be fragile, that is, easily damaged; or they may be robust, that is, not easily damaged; but it is also possible to take the spectrum further, and look for things that are antifragile, that benefit from stress, attacks, or the passage of time. Taleb gives the example from Greek myth of the Hydra, which grows two new heads each time one is cut off. What are your thoughts on this characteristic?

Lynn

Lynn, thanks for stretching my brain space again.

What would my boxing coaches say about Taleb's antifragile concept? In other words, if I had summarized the anti-fragile concept to them in a training session, what might they have said?

Reds Foley: "If you don't learn to move that head they'll soon be no room in there for those big ideas."

Big Rich: "No shit, Sherlock—give me another round!"

Raphael: "Steel sharpens steel. We don't sharpen our knives with silk pillows."

Mister Jimmy: "Some genius got paid for saying that? I wonder if he'll by my car. The transmission is shot."

Mister Frank: "That's the foundation of what we do here. I'd like to speak to this man. I'm sure I could learn something from someone smart enough to figure that out without stepping in the ring."

In other words Lynn, this is clearly known to anyone who has fought and who trains to fight or trains others to fight. There is all the equipment and technique to learn, the hundreds of rounds spent shadow boxing and meditating on method. However, one is not made fight ready until he is set to sparring with a partner.

That partner, if inept, and posing no danger to the fighter, will make this fighter weaker, will leach from him the essence he is trying to increase.

There are also numerous pitfalls to sparring, as many unproductive things that can crop up as productive ones. If sparring is mistaken for fighting, for instance, retardation and fixing of an incomplete skill set may occur. If conducted sensibly, sparring with the right sparring partner, which means a partner who poses some level of threat, is the only way one progresses in the training environment in such a way as to translate to the fight venue. But even this, since there are various takes on the behavior that fall short of the actual fight, only achieves a portion of a fighter's evolution.

Where the fighter gains mastery—the only place this occurs—is in that most dangerous setting where he can be stopped, injured, maimed or killed. Being stopped may cause a type of spiritual damage that is essentially an injuring, maiming or killing of the fighting spirit.

The fighter is brought along in evolutionary steps to prepare him first for an "antifragile" immersion in sparring and then finally in competition where the nature of the more lethal environment will greatly increase his adaptive quality.

This antifragile notion is, perhaps tied to Nietzsche's dictum, "That which does not kill us makes us stronger."

Admittedly, in the case of boxing, the coach is pre-selecting an antifragile—let's call him hyper-adaptive, though "robust" is really perfect, to be cultivated as an evolving combatant in progressively more stressful training sessions and then fights, in such a way that the fighter literally ascends a transformative field of experience, a field of experience ritually and perilously far beyond the domesticated norms of the civilized experience.

LL: James, you quote Nietzsche, whom Taleb discusses at length in the book, and in your last paragraph you note the importance of pre-selection on the part of the coach, another topic he covers extensively. It fascinates me to see intersections between seemingly disparate intellects, your insights particularly so, since you seamlessly combine both modes of inquiry, that of the mind and that of the body.

James, your piece makes me wonder what the world would be like if more boxers took up writing, or if writers took up boxing, or maybe if university professors were made to draw straws and fight to the death or lose tenure. Luckily, we have you!

JL: Lynn, interestingly there was once a world where all men boxed and hence learned lessons experientially which now require our very smartest men to address from a theoretical stance. I have no idea what my IQ is, but it's probably dismal. I really think that I only hit concepts that elude others because I've lived two life times, thanks to not sleeping, and now have the option of working fulltime as a writer. I do know numerous boxers who have aspired to writing, usually in fiction form, including John Coiley who writes music and has a novel published. It was once considered a no brainer that a writer had to box at some level. Louis L'Amour had a pro record with over 50 wins, I think. Robert E.

Howard loved boxing with his friends. My friend Oliver is a boxer with serious writing aspirations. Hemmingway was obsessed with boxing to the point where he wanted to spar with Jack Dempsey on a cruise, which horrified Dempsey, because he was afraid he'd damage the writer.

In Archaic and Classical Greece, where virtually all of our advanced military concepts, poetics and philosophy come from, all free men wrestled from early boyhood and boxed from age 12 to 16, unless they wished to pursue it further. Alexander called his fellow conquerors of the world—who won their battles on the mental plane, predominantly—"The Boys from the Gym."

As the greatest proponent of Hellenic masculinity ironically brought the aging civilization to its knees and passed on [323 B.C.] and a hundred years of mercenary empires took its place, birth rates dropped as did athletic participation, which became professionalized, as in our time. In 212 B.C. the last great Hellenic thinker Arkhimedes, was butchered by a Roman while doing an equation. Even so, the link between the life of the mind and the plight of the fighter was not altogether lost. Lyko of Troas [The Wolf of Troy, circa 150, I think] was a highly regarded philosopher who was known for boxing, even with professional champions.

Thanks for your line of questioning, Lynn. You've made me think.

Defeating the Perspective Trap

Lynn (LL) and James (JL) Discuss Three of Nassim Taleb's Antifragile Concepts

LL: I think you have applied this idea of antifragility in your own life quite extensively, especially the way that any aggression displayed against you is material for your writing. I often wonder what the learning process must have been like for you, much earlier in your life, as you developed your approach to managing the constant aggression in your environment. Can you comment on that?

JL: At age 11, after five years of being beaten and tormented by older children and teenagers, I talked my father into buying a punching bag and weight set and stayed inside until I could hit hard enough to make the floor above shake. The first ingredient a person needs to deal with aggression is the ability to apply aggression. You have to make at least one example before you can begin the nuanced threat negotiation that has typified most of my life. The sports comparison would be that you have to attain a certain baseline conditioning to engage in the sport in a learning way. By age 15 I had an aura of menace that kept almost everyone away. After nearly killing a man at 18 and narrowly avoiding prison time, I unlearned this, and had to learn it again on the job and on the way to work. By age 31, when I walked into a strip club—all 143 pounds of me—bouncers wanted to be my friend, businessmen would ask me to take their seats and the strippers would compete for my attention. This had only to do with the fact that I had become used to dealing with mobs of black youth and crews of gangbangers six nights a week and carried myself on a constant combat footing—was flat-out suicidal for most of my 30s. I had a D&D Charisma rating of 6 out of 18—just a bad actor who never initiated. The negroes could smell this, that I was like a coiled snake. I was really a creepy person who was utterly callous with everyone but my sons. My wife suffered greatly from this studied neglect of the softer parts of the world.

LL: Taleb has noted that he avoids anything or anyone that is "middle brow." He associates with only the most elite in any academic field, or taxi drivers, doormen, (and maybe grocers?). Back in 2008 he was getting death threats for his comments on the banks and markets and took up deadlifting to deter attacks. Now his deadlift is over 300 lbs. (he is in his late 50s with no previous athletic history). He loves hanging in the gym with the meatheads. He doesn't care for extensive proofreading of his writing, which is something he has in common with you. You specialize in mining the dregs of Baltimore for both your fiction and non-fiction. You have work to memorialize the lives of so many who served in unacknowledged slavery during the "colonial" era. Is it a coincidence that our elites wish to erase these classes of people who possess a type of understanding that has been effectively brainwashed out of the more compliant, educated classes?

JL: Okay, Lynn, you know how you continually take umbrage over my assertion that I'm a dumbass? Well, I am. I won't get into the years of crying as a child as I tried and failed to learn basic math, even with a tutor and remained unable to read two years after my younger brother was reading toy assembly instruction. Yet, the people in the middle of our society—you and most of my readers, who are college educated or brilliant laymen—are continually dumbfounded at how I can make deductions and observations that astound men such as Ulric Kerensky—who is a flat-out genius, I mean a dude who could have been a Tesla in another age, before the regimentation that drives minds like his underground. He calls it wisdom, what I have, and he is right. How did I get all of this insight that the big brains and beautiful minds gawk at and misunderstand?

I aspired to learn to read, and finally did. Made certain to read what others generally did not, history, anthropology, religion as well as the wars all boys read about. I did this so I could feel smart, not having the confidence to compete with others mentally in any way. Then, knowing myself unsuited for middle management, I stayed at the bottom of the bottom of the working class economy, a simple clerk in grocery stores for decades, refusing 13 offers of promotion as I slowly learned, and then finally learned that I was seeing that business from a perspective that no management person sees it from, as managers start on their track early and never gain deep experience at the low level. I had lower class perspective. When I finally agreed to a management job I held out for the top spot and got it, doing things that smarter, more experienced mangers—who could actually count money, for instance—could not do. I understood the engine that drove 60% of supermarket volume like no one else. I built a 7-man crew that carried a 110 person store out of failure and into profit.

Lynn, the people in the middle always suffer from lack of perspective—they are the meat, the grist of the social mill, the dupes and the fools. In early modern Britain, as the poor were being driven to the cities by the rural rich, where they were preyed upon my the Dickensian middle class, they formed an alliance with the urban old money, the heirs of fading fortunes and formed what was called "The Fancy" and came to be known as "the sporting set," in America. The men at the social apogee and at the social knee saw the world in like and ancient ways, where the herd, the flock, the fold of the merchant class and those aspiring to a place on its lower rung, clung to the merchant values that amounted to the worship of property and shunned all things spiritual, such as honor. The Fancy birthed prizefighting as the sport it is today, gangs of poor thugs and sets of dandies working as pug and sponsor, attendant and spectator to the fighters, their living mythic heroes, a thumb in the eye to the depraved middle class who campaigned for an end to prizefighting for over a century and failed. The middle class even fell like ducklings into the cult of celebrity born by boxing—with John L. Sullivan being the very first modern celebrity.

Men low and high saw that materialism was ultimately the death of humanity and gloried in risking health and fortune in a brutal imitation of the ancient heroes that had returned to the human imagination with the translation of Greek and Latin literature from the ancient world. Boxing literature from 200 years ago is chock full of ancient comparisons. The poor men played the hero to their fellows and betters as the smartest of the rich men read to them or wrote for them of the ancient heroes.

In short, Taleb figured out what I only learned through gross repetition and long years in the social depths he somehow framed in his imagination.

LL: Taleb has also introduced another concept -- skin in the game. This is probably the most important. He says you cannot trust anyone who does not take risks in their field. I can think of quite a few ways you exhibit this quality, and have therefore earned high credibility. For one thing, you write under your own name, in topics that are highly taboo, both to the ruling class and to some of the dissident groups. You are a pedestrian in possibly the most dangerous city in the US. You gave up your lucrative day job to write. I don't think there is a better example of skin in the game than your work on ancient weapons through *Modern Agonistics*. How can anyone believe a Ph.D. sitting in his office, when James LaFond has sacrificed blood and bone to learn the use of these weapons, in addition to your extensive reading?

JL: He re-introduced the oldest masculine aspect of tribal life into our sick world of leeches, wraiths and zombies. Lynn, now you know why I resist pleas to scamper to safety out of Baltimore, because skin in the game is all I really have that most literate humans lack, the source of my only real value as a non-fiction writer.

Now, the Ph.D. in his office cult that we have has real roots. Amongst the large brained creatures that make up my leadership [a Freudian typo I'm keeping since you people have pretty much led me around by the literary nose—I don't even decide what I read anymore. I'm like a crib-note generator for busy minds.], I probably fall on the short end of the scale in terms of brain power, but am swimming in a wealth of experience. Think of a more primitive society—like Big Ron's Baltimore—where the average knucklehead is nearly retarded and a fellow of mine and Ron's good but not great intelligence, becomes a sage or the guy with the right read on a situation while others get run over by a chain of events they may have initiated.

When everybody has the same experience, then being the Ph.D. is a big deal. This is the position of the coach in athletics. The intelligence of coaches over athletes is usually a larger spread than you'd see between management and labor. This, again, encourages high levels of adaptability in sports, with pro athletics outpacing most sciences in terms of adaptation of application, because you have brilliant coaches with a gut knowledge of the activity, communicating with the meatheads getting hit. Very few high-level athletes show any aptitude for coaching. So, where does the Ph.D. cult fit?

It fits in barrooms, in locker rooms, in a kick-ass Colonel's command center, that's why sports and war and beating the shit out of people, evolve and a democracy—a thing all about the collective center, about meat herders making the herd feel like they are serving it—has not changed since Athens.

Thanks for making me think this morning.

James

James, after reading a good deal of your work and having finished *Antifragile*, by Taleb, I have come to think of you as each other's alter egos, kindred spirits separated by place of birth, ethnicity, social castes and more. You have quite different intellectual affinities (Taleb is to math what LaFond is to combat arts) yet share insights relating to the human condition and history that are astonishing to me.

-Lynn

Mobi

My Country and My People: A Prequel to the Upcoming Matriarchy Article with Lynn Lockhart

Mobi is a LYFT driver who consented to speak with me for publication about the tribal structure of his nation and people. In the following section, Guerilla Patriarchy, Lynn grills me about the opinion of some Alt-Right thinkers that African, and by derivation African-American, cultures are matriarchal and powered by unique genetics. I led Mobi into this conversation for two reasons, first, to ask him about the Igbo people for a fellow writer and second, to see if he offers any information on the supposed matriarchal structure of his people and nation. Any misspellings in this are my mistake, as Mobi spoke and did not check my spelling. While discussing Nigeria in general and other tribes specifically, Mobi uses no hand gestures. When discussing America, his eyes grow wide with shocked sensibilities and his hands go inquiringly out to the side.

Working in America

The strangest aspect about coming to America is, that having been led to believe that America was a place of self-made people, one discovers that it is a place where men are passive in daily life—unless they are criminals—and that the women often behave as if they are men. Particularly in the city, the women are so assertive and so irrational that they are essentially insane. The primary characteristic of people in Baltimore is rudeness. The men ignore you and the women bother you, always in a rude manner. Even after I tell these much younger women that I am forty-five, they continue to express interest in me, like a man courting a woman. This is maddening. I say to myself, "Who does this? Who acts in this manner, but a crazy person?"

Of course, the lack of English in Baltimore is another aspect of the culture shock. One can say what he will about the English, and they have done some bad things, but they accomplished much and their language spans the globe. So, if one wishes to succeed, he speaks English, and well, not turning it into some kind of babble, but using it as a tool for self-advancement.

My Country

Nigeria was assembled by the British for their own purposes. The population consists of three tribes—with one sub-grouping associated with the Igbo. The Edo are placed under the Igbo, but are separate. They have just been categorized as a branch of that tribe. Lagos is the old capital, which has been replaced by Abuja for administrative, governmental purposes. However, Lagos is the center of economic life, of trade, of the movie industry. Lagos is the New York of Nigeria. All peoples come together there. It is on the coast, with Abuja inland.

The British left the Hausa tribe in charge. They are the largest group and span the northern reaches of the nation. It is they who contend with Boko Haram. The Hausa are mostly poorly educated and very poor. However, the elite of the nation are Hausa, who use their common people to extract vast wealth and amass power for themselves. The character of a Hausa man is one of quiet dignity, for he carries **the weapon**. Hausa men are known to go about armed. They tend to be polite and do not attempt to impose their ways or their will on the other tribes. The elite run the nation in a way that does not necessarily promote cultural interference. The Hausa man does not impose on you, for he has his weapon and his dignity and if you push him he will retaliate.

The Yoruba are numerous and not necessarily disruptive in any way. However, they are known to be hypocritical. The cab driver, Boomy, by his name, is a Yoruba man. The Yoruba man, has much in common with the Hausa man and the men of my people, for we are left to our own devices, to make our way through the educational system—or not—to acquire a trade and to forge ourselves. There is a lack of societies for men to grow strong in, and in that way, Nigeria is very much like America for the man, for he is adrift, in Life, in his own little boat.

With the Igbo man it is not so. The Igbo always thinks of his brother—"I must bring my brother along in my business, must teach my brother, must aid my brother."

This extends to the tribe. Every Igbo man will do first and foremost for his tribe and his fellow Igbo men. I know an Igbo man in Ownings Mills. He belongs to the Baltimore Igbo Caucus. In any city where Igbo men live, they have a caucus that meets regularly to discuss concerns for Igbo men, to promote the cause of Igbo culture, to promote Igbo business. I hear the Igbo Caucus in Houston is very strong. The Igbo are very irritating in that they meddle in the greater society, attempting to shape other peoples' culture in a way such as will suit their purposes. Igbo men are renowned as arrogant and tend to control business, are very much the bargaining merchant. The Igbo are very much like the Chinese, who have a presence in every country and do not alter their ways to conform to the native society and who tend to be business-oriented, meddlesome and arrogant wherever they go. In fact—and I did not understand this clearly until now—the Igbo in Africa are very much like the Jews in the United States, in that people in host countries complain of their meddlesome manner and would rather they not impose their culture and ways so aggressively.

My People

My late father passed away ten years ago. He had been sick and we thought, "He has always pulled through and he would this time as well."

Then, soon after I speak with him and hear his voice, confident of his strength, I receive the call that he has died. My father was an Edo man from Benin. Benin is a small, homogeneous nation beneath Nigeria, that was a French colony. Where the British loved to make nations of enemy tribes and group them together—for instance, Iraq, what is that but lines on a map ensuring contention?—placing one people over the others, the French—at least in Benin—had a more sensible situation.

My father never regarded himself as anything other than Nigerian. He moved to Nigeria when he was eight and he loved it as **his** country. After his death, I did visit Benin—one wants to know the place from where his father comes. In Benin I was suspected of being an Igbo, which is a hazard of being an Edo, people might think you are some meddlesome Igbo coming to tamper with their culture, to promote yourself and your people as superior, to peddle influence. A man misses his father. It is a terrible occurrence to be separated by distance, thinking he will be there to speak with and to learn of his death.

[*Speaks with a jutting jaw and strong but controlled gestures with the arm bent before the body and the hand half-opened and upward. The author confides that his father passed from life under identical circumstances.*]

My mother's people, they were Yoruba.

[*This statement, in response to the author's query about his matrilineal heritage, brings a slight snarl of disdain, and an abruptly dismissive back hand gesture. The author follows up with a question about masculine and feminine interaction in general. Mobi now uses chest thumping fingers to accentuate his statements below.*]

Women do not understand that a man must forge himself, must test himself against Life and grow in an assertive way. My mother says, "You should not drive in the city," and I say, "Mother, I will take a care. I will be fine. I must face adversity—I am a man."

They do not understand these things. But I am her son, so she must trust my judgment. It is simply her nature to worry.

My sister, she says, "How can you drive in the city with all of those insane people? You know they are mad."

I tell her, "A man must forge himself," and she does not understand.

[*Mobi continues on a subject more to his liking, again, with his upwardly expressive, coiled hand.*]

I know a man of Nigeria, a man of my people [Edo] who is writing a book of our history. His grandfather began this book, of the history of our people wherever we have gone. His father continued the book and still it was not complete, for it is the history of a people. Each country this man travels to and lives—such as Brazil—where our people have gone, he adds to the book and has plans on publishing it soon. He tells me that I can read the book and I look forward to this very much.

You are welcome, and have a good day in Baltimore.

[*Smiles*]

And so, in Baltimore, the theory of Universal Genetic African Matriarchy, in a land of a hundred kings, in the land of Nigeria where one king sold 14,000 slave girls to pay his passage to Mecca, in the lands of the Bantu, where naked men yet fight lions with lances, where Shaka Zulu shaped an iron age army that would defeat a modern one, where the kings of Swaziland and Dahomey have held thousands of wives and slave girls in sexual bondage, the idea of a race programmed for female domination wears thin.

Blood Sacrifice

A Discussion of Sacrifice in American Culture with James LaFond (JL) & Lynn Lockhart (LL)

LL: Taleb wrote a piece on lent, Easter, and blood sacrifice that I wanted to discuss with you. My thoughts were that the lack of blood sacrifice in Western religious practices is akin to the relinquishment of the individual's responsibility for violence to the State. No bloodshed means no spiritual life. When I read the King James Bible at age 19, one of the few things I was able to gather from it is that worshiping God in the Old Testament meant sacrificing to God. It did not mean singing songs while swaying in the church pew.

So far from requiring blood, or any effort whatsoever, most modern "non-denominational" Christian churches insist that there is nothing for Christians to do but say a few magic words and accept salvation. It never felt right to me.

JL: Lynn, there are so many varieties of new Christian churches that I cannot even address that subject, other than to say that these churches only remain vibrant for the first two generations. There is a constant branching by young Christians, making their own churches, even building them with their hands, in a never ending attempt to correct for the materialism that tends to creep so easily into church life.

My sister left the Catholic Church to join a first-generation church. In the Catholic Church, as a boy, I was exposed to the gay, light-rock, feel-good, hippie version of New Age Catholicism and even at age eight, saw it is a phony attempt to make religion cool for kids. There is, in Catholicism, a focus on sacrifice and the symbolism of blood, but the only sacrifice asked by the priest is the donation. I recall my parents being humiliated when their two dollar donations were posted in the church weekly, next to those made by business owners and CEOs. This is where religion always ends up and that is why American Christians have reformed as young churches constantly, for the four centuries of our continually fracturing history.

In the Appalachian and rural piedmont churches I have attended, the notion of sacrifice seems to focus on not taking the many pleasures that the gross world offers—a post monastic form of abstinence that fits well in such a pleasure-saturated society and I think makes a good surrogate for bleeding. The better postmodern churches are, in a sense, fertile monasteries.

Also, there is still a crusading notion among rural Christians who make up the bulk of U.S combatants in its money-grubbing wars, a notion I see as being exploited by the globalists, but is authentic none-the-less in the minds of many, who see themselves as holding back The Caliphate.

The musical orientation of some of the money-focused, feel-good churches you mention reminds me of the black ghetto churches in Baltimore, which manage to concentrate money and sexual access in the person of a store front minister. The only sacrifice being made in these churches is the woman's gift of her oft-sampled sexual goods to the neighborhood patriarch, who stands as the alternative to the other two patriarchs in the black community: the drug king pin and White Daddy [government].

Traditionally, in American Protestantism, the notion of sacrifice has been Abrahamic, in that sons were sacrificed to the wars of expansion that spread the Gospels among the Heathen and that the lives of the early plantation Congregationalists in New England were literally sunk into the alien soil in their effort to eradicate the native forest ecology and replace it with a grassland. In 1868, Meshach Browning recalled that he had done his Christian duty by siring a family of 64 sons, grandsons and great grandsons, who stood ready to fight for his nation—an overtly Christian nation.

Aside from the sacrifice of sons in war and the more heroic sacrifice of oneself [which has never been the preferred American sacrifice, sons being favored over self], the protestant ethic of toil, or doing what a man can to live a virtuous life on an evil earth is almost Roman in character. The best example of this would be the ploughing scene in *Sergeant York,* where the hero, played by Gary Cooper is shown working the land, literally attacking the rugged natural environment.

In respect to sacrifice, in American culture, the notion among Catholics has been completely farmed out to the past, of Jesus taking the full burden. The aspects of sacrifice are revered, but they are not for men. This has really caused the guilt-rot to emerge strongly in American Catholicism, with third world immigrants and even Islam—the religion—being embraced as suffering foci for the post-suffering American Catholic. Currently joint Islamic-Catholic services are being held in Baltimore, and old Catholics, like my mother and aunt are being guilted into sitting through Spanish mass next to Mexicans carrying baby dolls in coffins. In this fashion the elder women in my family act out the simpering sacrifice of identity before the altar of their all-erasing God.

I suspect that the above notion of guilt-based sacrificed, of living prosperously as the benefactors of an ancient God's suffering, lingers even in the secular, ethical construct of American Atheism, wherein a nominally Christian person, secularized beyond redemption, is led to believe that his abstinence from actual sacrifice can be atoned for by sacrificing his unborn children via omission, and stepping aside in sterile old age as the suffering slave classes from Latin America and beyond takes the places at the American Table of the Last Supper that might have been occupied by his children.

The turning point for me, is the year of my birth, 1963, and the Yul Brynner movie *Kings of the Sun*, with Shirley Anne Field and George Chakiris. Brynner plays a proto-Comanche Indian chief who at first opposes, then allies with, a fleeing Mayan King and his exiled people. The king, played by Chakiris, at one point overrules the high priest in the matter of sacrifice, noting that this new land was so fertile that no sacrifice need be made. [This is a heavily propagandistic story line aimed at indigenous white America.] In the end, the sacrifice is made on the temple stairs, when the native chief, played by Brynner, dies defending the refugees from their pursuing enemies on the very stairs of the un-bloodied sacrificial pyramid. In the year of my birth a movie maker was already preaching what the new Christian sacrifice would be in America, the extinguishing of identity and patrimony, in favor of refugees from across the sea.

To get back to your objection to "singing songs and swaying in the church pew" as a form of religious expression that has replaced sacrifice, I might add that available evidence hints at conversion to Christianity of black slaves by their white masters as facilitated more easily by indulging the African penchant [which does, indeed, seem to be genetic] for song and dance. Again, the sacrificial aspect of toil is present, as it was through the entire Middle Ages, when the suffering serf carried the fighting and praying classes on his back in return for the promise that his way to eternal paradise had been assured by the sacrifice of Christ.

In summation, it is my opinion that in the Western World, with all of its indigenous traditions submerged by Christianity and with Christianity itself fighting off cycle after cycle of corruption introduced by the rampant materialism of modernity, that the notion of sacrifice remains three-tiered as it always has: work from the poor, money from the merchant, blood from the powerful and their pawns and offered with words from the ruling class.

The latter has three postmodern manifestations:

1. The powerful, and those of a liberal mind who align themselves with the elite, by and large, sacrifice their bloodline to their post-Christian ideology, by forgoing reproduction and adopting suffering groups and individuals as their children, in this way retaining much of the psychology of sacrifice.

2. The massive, secular edifice of modernity—in its America form—has retained a Christian patina, with mottos such as, "In God We Trust," and "One Nation Under God," not yet stricken from the American creed, encouraging predominantly Christian

combatants to sacrifice their lives in the "The War on Terror."

3. Every day, in every mid-sized to large city in America, the thugs of the Black Urban Mobs that have risen since 2014, are shedding the blood of those who must bleed and die for the crime of being born white. Among the victims one will see a strong tendency not to blame their attackers, a common aspect of sacrificial victim behavior.

Thank you, Lynn.

James, thank you for this outstanding piece. You have, once again, surprised me with the direction that you have taken my inquiry, and the depths you explore. You have identified ways in which Americans sacrifice, going back into our history, even in this most materialistic society. It seems an intrinsic human trait, that is bound to express itself, in a way offering hope for the survival of the human spirit.

-Lynn

Lynn, I do think that the human willingness to sacrifice will offer hope as long as we remain human. In the near term, however, I am afraid that most thinking people in the Western World have elected to sacrifice their bloodline on the myriad altars of the God of Things, as I term materialism, a manmade force that seems to have accumulated more worshippers than any of the many version of supernatural God we have managed to address.

In the long term, we must be on the lookout for the sure-to-come attempts to gather human reproduction as corporate resources, with the ultimate goal being the sterilization of humanity into nothing more than meat-puppets.

Thanks for the hard question.

A Breathing Bandage for the Fatherless Soul

Discussing Guerilla Patriarchy with Lynn Lockhart

James,

Recently, Zman, a fellow Baltimore denizen of yours, gave an interview with Kevin Michael Grace which you shared on your site.

The following exchange takes place beginning 17:50 (I transcribed this myself, please excuse any errors):

KMG: What do you hear about the matriarchy?

Zman: There's no question, and I think that would never change. I think there is something there that goes back a lot farther than modern history, you talk to people who grew up in Africa, there is a guy on my blog who is originally from Rhodesia, and he will tell you that in Sub-Saharan Africa, it's a female dominated society. There is a narrow role for males, but the domestic life, community life is largely dominated by females and I think there is a biological component there, that transcends anything that we are going to do as a society.

Steve Sailer has made similar observations, including an amusing excerpt on behalf of the African matriarchy theory, from the book The Marriage Problem, by James Q Wilson, Vox Day has expressed similar thoughts, and even your unpaid intern seems to think so.

James, what can you tell us about the life-ways and habits of Baltimore's African diaspora with regard to matriarchy, patriarchy, or some unholy sociological innovation?

-Lynn

White Daddy and His Bitch

Lynn, in Baltimore what you have is not a matriarchy, but a decapitated patriarchy, cast aside to permit the mutated matriarchy to interface with the meta-patriarchy: The State, known by blacks as The Man and White Daddy.

Hoodrat mothers cast aside would-be men in order to marry the State and then behave as experimental female-beastmen, brutalizing their boys from the cradle to the jailhouse and allowing both boys and girls under their roof to be raped by male relatives and the sex drones that serve her. It is a nightmare, with neither a functional patriarchy nor matriarchy, a broken society. An anthropologist has called this bureaugamy, husbandless women married to the bureaucracy.

But what about the female dominated political machine in black urban centers?

This is simple, black men may not vote because they are almost all felons, because their mothers raise them in an argumentative and brutal fashion which weirdly requires them to fight the cops as a rite of passage. Even if they were just jaywalking, fighting the cops turns it into a felony. There are hardly any black male voters.

Yesterday I walked by a welfare queen in a nice neighborhood, standing in the doorway with her black paramour, scolding her two children by different men, one a mulatto and the other an octoroon like her. She beat the five year old boy brutally before me and the assembled neighbors, the child screeching in horror as the powerless black youth she is dating—a third her weight—cringed in the doorway, and as the boy of another, lighter-skinned man writhed on the porch.

Lynn, this is a mutilated matriarchy running amok as the decapitated patriarchy lies in the gutter. That black stud was cringing—I am guessing—at the memory off his own mother beating him like his giant mistress beat the spawn of a previous drone.

Before going into examples of African patriarchy, let me state why the Zman and Vox Day, both brilliant men, cannot understand matriarchy or patriarchy: They are, as is our entire society, critically emasculated.

Matriarchy and Patriarchy

They, and even our anthropologists, generally look at a society as either matriarchal or patriarchal. That is a grave error that disables any understanding of human gender dynamics. This comes from the fount of Western Civilization, the pastoral takeover of agrarian civilization by conquering nomads.

Before describing that, let me back up further.

Patriarchy is a paternal hierarchy, a masculine order.

Matriarchy is a maternal hierarchy, a feminine order.

Any healthy society has within it a functional matriarchy and a functional patriarchy, two human spheres that interact, ideally in an overlapping fashion, not a clashing fashion and not in a submerging manner.

Traditionally, for hundreds of thousands of years, the matriarchy dominated the camp, the cave, the home and the patriarchy dominated interaction with the natural world and with other societies. This is exemplified in Amerindian traditions such as the Iroquois, whose men owned nothing but their weapons and whose women shared political power and owned all household goods.

Back to this later, as this is the crux of the book *A Dread Grace*, the thesis of which is that shared gender power is the basis for hyper-aggressive war-making men, such as the Spartans, the Zulus, the Iroquois, et al.

Matriarchal Submersion

When one gender sphere is squashed or submerged by the other we have an unhealthy society. In traditional, Middle Sea Based [Roman, Semitic, Hellenic] Societies, where nomad conquerors had completely crushed lesser tribes, the status of free manhood was denied conquered men and they were driven into the household as its close master, now squashing the matriarchy under them as they became hairy women. Upon meeting Western Settlers, Amerindians rarely identified European men as men, but as mutilated women, for they farmed and stayed housebound, not hunting and journeying and raiding, but behaving like native women. In this situation, the civilized woman becomes a slave in the same house that a barbarian woman would have ruled, forcing her man to range far and wide and deal with the world rather than huddle womanlike in his false castle.

Patriarchal Decapitation

Ron West, adopted member of the Blackfeet people, calls his people matriarchal, as that is their anthropological designation and we westerners who labeled them so see and shared power between the matriarchal and patriarchal spheres as matriarchal—or female dominated. In reality, according to Ron's own history of the tribe, the Blackfeet men were not the slaves and servants of the women, but shared equally the powers of the tribe. Then the whites came and split the chiefs between loyalists and drunken puppets and their Jesuit priests went directly for the women and converted them to Christianity, which was how the Catholics originally converted the Germanic kings, by getting to the queen first, which was allowed, because civilized and monkish men were regarded by both red and white barbarians as effectively female and allowed access to the women, who, since they occupied an honored place next to the men, had equal influence, which was enhanced by the fact that the men had been split by drug addiction and venomous diplomacy. Thus the natural men find that half of their number have been seduced by the Whiteman's drugs and that their women have been seduced by his religion and are separated from the community. This is further exacerbated by the fact that the men now face irrelevance in their manly sphere, for a handful of stone age warriors—even super warriors—cannot fight the machine arm of a million man state and no longer have game to hunt, or the freedom to range widely and are thus left with nothing.

There is essentially no difference in how the Indian or the black man have been emasculated by white civilization. Each Indian tribe had its own story and own masculine death and many have managed a revival, have managed to grab back some ground only to have modern feminism hit them between the eyes.

Black men were originally set aside as the white slave master bred his woman to produce half-breed slaves. After emancipation it took almost a hundred years before black families really began to form. According to Patrick Buchanan in the 1950s, black families were "more churched" than white. According to Thomas Sowell, black men had significantly closed the income gap between 1954-55.

Then, in 1964, LBJ unleashed a plan to destroy the formed-from-scratch black family by initiating State-to-Mother macro-marriage and casting the black man out of the house he had taken a hundred years to build. The process accelerated demonically due to these factors:

1. Not coming from a western, submerged matriarchy, but from Africa, where the gender spheres tend to coexist at a level of separation most reminiscent of the classical Hellenic household, in which men hardly socialized with their wives, who kept separate quarters, people of predominantly African decent are already predisposed to gender separation. The numerous African men I speak to, speak of brothers, fathers and other men of their tribe

or nation, not of their mothers, wives and lovers as emasculated Americans of all colors will speak.

2. Not having fully assimilated to the greater American society, cultural disintegration was more likely under such stress.

3. The civil rights movement largely promoted feminist values in a communistic context and came to favor female leadership. One recent example is of the two black female mayors of Baltimore, who have looked to their presidents as father figures and have been petulantly overruled by their white male governor on crime matters. This fatherless-daughter-as-municipal-executive-worshipful of the federal "White Daddy" [I know black women who even called Obama "White Daddy'] was never better illustrated than when Stephanie Rawlings-Blake was told by Eric Holder of the Justice department to stand the police down and she did, as her male underlings seethed with rage. She was eventually trumped by the Whiteman governor who sent in the National Guard. In the end, a female mayor is nothing but a slaughter at big daddy's knee.

4. The low intelligence and high defiance of black criminal youth ensured that most urban black men would never become voters, causing an unbalance between the patriarchy and the matriarchy in the black population, which, to be clear, does not represent a separated community from the white population, but merely an underclass. The only sense

of community in the back population is found in the Guerilla Patriarchy.

Guerilla Patriarchy

The black population has been shattered out of community and into social atomization. If one wonders why blacks, as a rule, are fawned over by globalists and the media, it is because the former black community, rendered now into the black underclass, ordered from raped toddlers and shivering addicts in cardboard boxes at the bottom to rappers and athletes and false-maternal icons like Oprah at the top, was the test project for the mono-cropping of humanity, a racially homogeneous, purely class-based mass of unaligned individuals. You whites should look at black America now for a glimpse into the future that has been planned for you. This is meant to be the fate of all peoples, all races, atomization, the division and conquest of society on a subatomic level.

Blacks in American cities call the federal government and the state and municipal tiers and armies of cops, lawyers, social workers and medical persons who are an ever-present hand of unseen but always-felt power in their daily lives The Man and White Daddy, expressions that hark back to the antebellum plantation and before that the English servant plantation, which was ruled by one man, as one

Virginia slave master of 1711 put it, "like a biblical patriarch of old."

This leaves a deep yearning for a flesh and blood daddy figure in the lives of lonely black women and their children. I have had numerous blacks adopt me as their White Daddy, over a hundred at last count and this is often the social role of the boxing coach in urban environments, a breathing bandage for the fatherless soul.

There is another patriarchy, one that is under our noses, bloodying it all the time but remaining unrecognized due to our abysmal, emasculated ignorance.

This is the Guerilla Patriarchy found in various forms. Always extremely, almost cartoonishly, male-dominated and oriented, the postmodern black-identity street gang is an extreme patriarchy, an ephemeral cipher of a society dedicated to the creation and financing of black men—even at the cost of dying before age 35 as most do. This gang activity, exemplified by The Black Guerilla Family (BGF), the name of the most prominent Baltimore area gang, is an extreme reactionary social symptom one may expect from the body sub-politic that remains after the patriarchal structure of a culture has been decapitated. This dynamic actually informed my writing of *Reverent Chandler* and *Malediction Song*. This dynamic, the Guerilla Patriarchy is what The Wolves of Vinland and other such neo-barbarian hyper-masculine groups are practicing, albeit in a more sophisticated if less successful way than the BGF and other black identity gangs.

Note that gangster life is distantly modeled on white, Irish criminality in similar urban centers and that, like the Irish before them, the blacks are penetrating law enforcement as well.

Hallmarks of black identity gangster life include the rejection of "government names" in favor of street-names, including the mother's pathetic attempts to invent an atomized identity for her son by giving him a lisping name of pseudo-Arabic inspiration.

Conclusion

Yes there is a black matriarchy, a malformed social order put in place and utterly beholden to Uncle Sam himself for the purpose of extinguishing and suppressing African-American patriarchy.

As emasculated-in-the-cradle civilized Americans, the Zman (who declines to express his counter cultural opinion under his real name) and Vox Day, brilliant men though they may be, look at a society such as the many in Africa, where men and women live gender-based lifeways instead of being two-gender Siamese twins like American married couples, and see in this natural, ages old, universally human separation of gender roles and function as matriarchy, largely because the mutilated remains of America Indian tribes whose patriarchal structure had been negated and superseded by the paternal federal government, labeled such societies matriarchal.

We see also, in nations like Sweden and Germany, where the State has turned to a mothering role, an upwelling of the matriarchal urge to be dominated by a very different person—with the majority of women in such places obviously preferring, based on voting outcomes and behaviors, to be gang raped by foreign men than to be served by domestic men.

Achilles and Odysseus, Gilgamesh and Enkidu, Roland and Beowulf, Sitting Bull and Crazy Horse, would look today at the postmodern American man, who cares more for the company of his wife than for his fellows as some kind of freak of nature, somehow unable to understand that men and women work best together when they remain different and then come together and join as mates, achieving the overlapping of the divergent spheres of femininity and masculinity.

Both the traditional Western perversion of placing the man in the house as the slave of God [See Leviticus] and lord of the woman and the current practice of making of the man a monster and all things masculine monstrous—unless clothed in the flesh of denatured womanhood, are equally distorting and perverse of the natural order of man and woman, protector and nurturer of what is human.

The black rejection of democracy in favor of strong men in Africa and Haiti and of gang life in America, represents a visceral distrust of democratic politics, as democracy is womanish in all of its squawking aspects, encouraging men to squabble like women and amounting to a popularity contest to determine who gets to aim the Great Gun of State, rather than a trial by danger.

Notes on African Patriarchy

1. African men I speak to almost never speak of the mother or wife without apologizing for rudely inserting a woman into the discussion. Boomy, my cabbie friend, is in charge of checking homework and report cards for his daughter, the wife having no authority here. He and other Nigerian men are very patriarchal in outlook. Mobi regarded his mother and her tribe as unimportant to his formation as a man and resents her Americanized meddling with his daughter.

2. In fractured American and Americanized black populations like in Baltimore and Liberia, rape by black men is experienced by over 80% of black females, representing a seething animosity toward the forced false matriarchy of the husbandless mother backed by the meta-patriarchy of the State.

3. African queens were less numerous than European queens, had fewer powers and were less

warlike than kings, where European queens were more warlike than their kings. The Queen of Uganda was a gigantic fertility goddess that drank milk all day long and had to be rolled around and bathed by attendants. The explorer John Hanning Speke measured her rear end and thighs like a farm animal with no complaint made by her king or people.

4. The Masai are and were dominated by lion-hunting warriors and their women adore them like kings.

Photo credit: Old East Africa Postcards

5. The Zulu kings forbade their young men to have intercourse with their wives-to-be until they had fought in a battle.

6. The Haitian slaves that rose up in the wake of the French revolution rejected the Rights of Man and wished to fight under a king. One, Mimeca, dictated a letter to the effect that he was a warrior and had fought under three kings, one of the Congo, one of

France and one of Spain, and would not accept a collective notion of rule.

7. The famous Amazons of the West African KINGDOM of Dahomey were 5,000 wives of the king, subject to his patriarchy and bearing his children but otherwise permitted to live as men, shouldering arms in the field on his behalf and taking a wife to care for their household and child. This is, in all aspects, a patriarchal arrangement.

8. The current King of Swaziland has numerous wives at his disgusting disposal—hardly a matriarchal arrangement.

9. Hip Hop, or gangster rap, is a vicious attack on matriarchal notions, a feral, woman-hating reveling in unilateral male dominance, and is the single most influential cultural contribution to American public life made by Americans of African descent.

Photo credit: some hip hop album

10. Kangs and Queens is a strong motif in Hip Hop culture. Any man who has bedded black women, as I have, knows that they are slaves to the male penis even more so than the famously slutty white women of the hipster and millennial generations. Once you dick a black woman she is your slave until you cast her off, and then she is your most murderous enemy. Most black women abandon their children for hours on end to be inseminated by random men, but preferably Gangster Kangs and White Daddies: clear patriarchal figures. Most food stamp money spent in Baltimore is dedicated to the feeding of luxury meats to the temporary king in her dubious bed, while her children eat cheap hot dogs and ramen noodles. This is not patriarchy or matriarchy, but a symptom of the grasping grossness of a psychologically mutilated people, attempting to purchase some parody of kingship and queenship—some balanced joining in the shadow of the system that has denatured them so coldly—with the bribe that bought their humanity.

Civilization is Evil.

James, this is a powerful piece, revealing and framing the mechanism that has undone Western culture. Hegel would be gratified to read your take on the question of matriarchy vs. patriarchy. University trained anthropologists or sociologists will get stuck on questions of paternal certainty, private property and accumulation of technology. Libertarians, and their hatred of government, will be confused about why they agree with you (they also often hate defined gender roles). There are many flavors of patriarchy, and of matriarchy, but the ones we have now are a complete failure.

-Lynn

Lynn, in the interest of full disclosure, I have only seen Hegel's name in the tables of contents of books on philosophy that I could never complete, as social thinking past Hobbes simply bored me. So I suspect vaguely that he was some smart Kraut. I'm not going to google him and pretend I read him.

In the interest of piling on, here are some African Patriarchy items:

-Mobi, the Nigerian Lyft driver who is a good friend of Lili's and mine, said of the way African American women dress when they get into his car, "If a young woman dressed like that in Nigeria the men of the area would surround her and shame her, punish her for being so forward and humiliating her family."

-There was an African tribe in which the men elongated their wives' necks by placing stacked rings around them. If she was unfaithful, the rings were removed and her atrophied neck would snap.

-Female "circumcision" is not Islamic [Arabic] in origin, but had its roots in Northeast Africa among blacks.

-When adventuring in Northeast Africa, Richard F. Burton noted that one tribe's men pierced and laced their wives' labia closed before leaving her at home.

-My friend Oliver returns to visit his grandmother in Jamaica to make sure that no men have been taking advantage of her in business dealings. He also cares for his mother and sisters, providing them with cars while he drives junkers, giving his sister a place to live, etc. Disappointed in his father's level of familial commitment he has made of himself the patriarch of a family, hardly suggesting that African folk are genetically doomed to matriarchal-dominated society.

-Recently, Lili told me that a Nigerian man brought his sister into the tag and title service and gave his sister a car, which she claims is the opposite among our indigenous blacks, who typically practice female-to-male transfers. This, and the fact that Mobi has recently decided to pay half of his sister's mortgage, might be regarded as suggestive of culturally transmitted African traditions that have broken down in America.

-As a grocery store manager, I worked closely, for three years, with a Ghana man who could never get a handle on American female behavior. He could look upon them as "Madam" the female owners, or as my property [seriously, if he saw me talking to a female customer, he mentally tagged her as mine and considered her off limits], or as his. He called me Boss constantly, never using my name, even when speaking to others. I was "the Boss," "Boss" or "Bossman," indicating that ideas of male hierarchy had a strict and powerful hold on his mind, extending, even into his past. Young Ghana men would seek him out at the store for advice and he would introduce them to me as good prospects but currently undeserving of direct words with me. His former employer he introduced to me in admiring tone, informing me, "Boss, you are my boss, but Mister John will always be my boss." John was the man that gave him his first American job and who, upon hearing that I was considering his former man for employment, took timeout to come and meet me, assuring me that I was hiring a good man.

-The above reminds me of the German observations that African men, if led properly and with respect, made excellent war fighters, with a tiny cadre of German officers and their African troops consistently defeating superior English-Officered African and Anglo-Indian troops in "Operation Side Show," during World War I, indicating that African men might have benefited more from strong patriarchal leadership of the Teutonic type than the womanly troop management style of the British aristocracy.

Well, Lynn, that's all I can scrape off the top at the moment.

Thanks for assembling this case for my commentary.

The Artifice of Fatherhood

Lynn Lockhart and James Discuss the Masculine Role

James, recently you recounted your experiences of being targeted for aggression based on your female company in *Amping up the Race Hate*. You stated there, as you have before, that were it not for "the artifice of being a father," you would be making headlines as an example of the need for knife and stick control, to stop heterosexual white men from murdering innocent youths (I am paraphrasing).

James, I think you are not being quite fair to yourself here, in light of your role as a father, and the importance of the father in the family and in society. This recalls our discussion on matriarchy and patriarchy, because what most alt-right people mean by patriarchy is a society where paternal investment in their offspring is high. By and large, you don't get high investment from men without ensuring paternal certainty, and this is where oppression of women comes into the picture (don't shoot me, I am just the messenger).

Fatherhood is not an artifice, in fact, it might be the essence of humanity. First, in the basic Darwinian sense, if you don't have descendants, you may as well have never existed. Second, and more importantly, paternal investment in young is rather rare in the natural world and varies greatly among human societies. Long story short, more paternal investment is better.

James, our families are the first line of defense against alienation. Your sons stand between you and the world burnt to a cinder, but they also stand between you and a totally unmoored and atomized existence, short though it may be. Thank them for me.

-Lynn

Lynn, in the strictest sense I believe fatherhood is artifice, social artifice. In this materialistic world where art and artifice have been turned into baubles, masks, lies, moral straightjackets, etc., we may think of artifice as bad, as it so often is, but fatherhood, and the entire suite of psychological disciplines that make up successful human societies are social adaptations to a very primal fact.

When we become adults we have two opposite experiences: A woman is transformed into a life giver.

What does a boy transform into?

The boy becomes a lethal version of his former self, a person typically possessing the ability to take life in a way previously barred to him. A typical man, or vigorous youth, has the ability to kill children, women and the elderly with his bare hands.

This is an event of potentially catastrophic outcome for the tribe. If these youth are not taken away from the vulnerable portion of the population and indoctrinated into a moral order then humanity gets what civilization has given it, a social substrata of savage, feral youth who have emerged in the absence of the fathering process and the process of masculine tribal societies, which have been replaced by naked proxy force, replaced by the police state, which teaches its own brutal lesson.

Fatherhood, manhood, warriorhood, these are all socially generated artifice. Manhood is much less instinctual than womanhood and more sensitive to materialistic artifice. Such mechanisms as states supersede fatherhood–often with mothering constructs [alternative artifice] –and cast male youth into a savage incubator of feral minds, incapable of surviving in a traditional natural band, in a traditional tribal context or in highly evolved masculine societies who were once the core of social stability for both tribes and nation states. However, once the nation uncoupled from the state, masculine societies had to be jettisoned, for they would produce an organic–superior–social artifice in the form of manhood, rather than an employee, a debtor or a voter.

Thanks, James, for another thought provoking response. I hadn't considered that artifice might have neutral or even positive connotations. This opens the door to exploring those layers of civilized behavior that are beneficial, and the Taboo Man's approach to them.

Until next time...

-Lynn

Lynn, in many ways our perceptions of organic human tradition have been so warped by the semantics foisted upon us in our youth, that discussions like this are necessary for our sustenance and must be necessarily denied to the mass of humanity, ideally through state education and commercial media, in order that we might be fruitfully harvested by our planters.

A Captive Woman's Gall

Lynn and James Discuss Online Handles

James,

You recently linked to Kevin Michael Grace's interview of a fellow with the handle "Jay Fivekiller." From listening to the interview, one can gather that J-5 is something of a neighbor of mine, in the San Francisco metro area. You included the following comment, which has caused me to stew since then, since I am also guilty of using a pseudonym:

"Like it or not, Jay Fivekiller and other anonymous Alt-Righters do not value their opinion as highly as whatever money they are making."

This is particularly galling for me, because I don't even make any money, and I hardly express any opinions here, I mostly just ask you questions!

Then recently, ten once-and-future privileged oppressors had their admissions to Harvard rescinded for posting inappropriate memes in what they thought was a private Facebook page. This quote had me rolling around laughing:

"Harvard does not comment on individual applicants' admission statuses, but incoming students are explicitly told upon receiving an offer that behavior that brings into question their moral character can jeopardize their admission."

There are many other examples, notably Brendan Eich, who created a major software language, was fired from his post as CEO of Mozilla when it was leaked that he donated to support traditional marriage.

James, the persecution is real, and many of us in the bourgeoisie are barely hanging on, even with six figure salaries. It takes a lot of courage to write under your own name, as you do, and it is no small thing to structure your life in such a way that neither your livelihood nor your loved ones can be taken hostage.

-Lynn

Lynn, my statement as to the men who write under pen names stands, they care more about remaining in the bosom of their beloved and wrathful God of Things than they do about their convictions, ideals–their souls.

However, you are not a man, but a woman, so you get a pass.

The use of the pen name to protect women in the male-dominated realm of the published word is at least as old as Mary Shelly and her Modern

Prometheus. I suspect, though that females assuming a protective identity [for instance Einstein not having done his own work, but depending on his wife] goes as far back as *The Odyssey*, which is attributed to Homer, but which I and other readers suspect might have been composed by a woman, perhaps his daughter.

Marriage, for instance, has often cloaked a woman's identity in the protection of her husband's identity. When I moved to Baltimore and interviewed for a supermarket job, the person who hired me, Miss Betty, broke a long-standing agreement with her husband, that they hired their own gender only. He was quite offended that she hired me and gave me a hard way to go. She, however, reminded him that, "this is my business Leonard–you're the picture on the box, I'm the cereal." Mister Len was strictly relegated to handling the money and being the male face of the business while his wife ran the show.

This is just one example.

Another exemption from my scathing critique is the family man, men like Ishmael, Shayne, Mescaline, and so many others who have vulnerable family who are in business, or raising small children, and who need to be sheltered from the social war by people who take the pre-doxed stance that I, Jack Donovan, Greg Johnson, and other people who write and publish under our own names, do.

This is how men behave tribally. Certain men will paint the bulls-eye on themselves and carry on the discourse, suffer the alienation, etc., while their supporters secretly agree, slip them resources, and bide their time while they try to raise children who will not become sucked into the vortex of evil. This is–tribally speaking–a shamanic role, placing oneself outside the social construct and off the hierarchical path, in order to be able to express a dissenting view. Unknown by many, people in power, even those who pursue evil, value this function as a progress marker and don't seek to wipe out a dissenter who is not on the hierarchical-economic track.

I have been told by many readers that they support me because I speak for them where they would be destroyed or put out of work for expressing an honest opinion.

My slave girl won't even let her children know my last name for fear she would be ostracized for associating with such a fiend as I.

My older son is a mechanic, in a trade, and immune to his association with me.

My younger son has long wanted to be a CEO or CFO of a large company. We decided that he should begin writing grant letters for college claiming poverty by insanity, as his father had quit a management job to become a science-fiction novelist. He started his public separation from my opinion at age 18. He even discusses me with his coworkers, who seem to regard me as some sort of Neanderthal ho-macking, demi-god. Basically, even in a corporate environment he has been honest with his associates and the men above him in stating that, "my dad is essentially crazy, still fights young jocks, takes the bus in Baltimore city, grosses less annually than I pay in taxes in the first quarter, but is a lot of fun and can kick just about all my friends' asses... I have absolutely no desire to be like him, but he's a great guy to have around and gives me great advice on soft skills that he learned managing a workplace full of ex-convicts."

So, Lynn, for people like Jay Fivekiller, Paul Kersey, Zman and the various authors I used to follow at Return of Kings and Eradic, who write under pen names, I suspect, that when the rubber hits the road, they will fold and denounce themselves and their fellows, because this society has effectively emasculated them in the crucible of comfort that is Modernity. This is the normal state for a woman, who must denounce her man to save her children.

An example comes from a Tennessee settlement in the 1700s, which was under siege by a superior Indian force. The wives of the few remaining men told their husbands to leave. If the men stayed and fought the outcome would be the same, they would become Indian wives and their children would be raised as Indians. They wanted to be spared seeing their husbands killed and did hold out hope that their husbands might eventually mount a raid to get them back or even raise a ransom. They were confident that the largely white Indians would treat them and their children well and knew that there would be a horrible end for their men. Women have had to function like this through all of our formative ages and it is ingrained. Continue to protect yourself, Lynn, it is what a woman living under enemy occupation or in captivity does.

Thanks for expressing your gall, Lynn.

James.

P.S. People in my position who have stepped beyond the pale, do not wish to see our supporters targeted. I would rather be attacked by antifa faggots than have one of my readers doxed.

James,

Thanks for the girl pass! I like to think I hold myself to the same standards as men, but now is as good a time as any to let that conceit go. I think I am a little more optimistic than you, I think the alt-right is building support and I have seen some who plan to double down if they are ever exposed. Even here, deep in enemy territory, there is a surprising concentration of dissenters, though most remain masked.

Thanks for the exchange, James,

Lynn

'A Young Man Starting Out?'

A Man Question from J on Pen Names

Commenting on *A Captive Woman's Gall.*

So pen names are justified in the case of protecting families.

But would you recommend a young man starting out stay outside the hierarchy, or adopt a pen name and focus on family?

-J

J, I'm flattered you would ask me this.

First, the pen name has practical earning uses. Vox Day basically uses a pen name that is a catchy handle, a branding effort. If you want to write in broad categories, like I do, but not ruin your fiction appeal by writing unpopular opinions, as I have, a publisher would prefer you write under two different names.

J, I am thrilled—and I am sure so is Ishmael and the other old coons that read here on the site—that you are considering a family. Once one has decided on a family, if you want to plant your seed against the degenerate grain of our warped society, then family comes first. Traditional hierarchies incorporated the family. Modern hierarchies subvert the family and atomize the person.

A family requires a certain number of dollars to thrive in this world, so stay out of corporate settings. Going into business for yourself is fraught with risk, so consider working in a trade of some kind. Your hierarchal relationships should be religious, athletic, sporting, artistic, etc.

If you just make the money to keep a temporary family and then watch your children dispersed into the atomized world, like I have, you will find yourself standing at the edge of a yawning abyss. I surrendered my sons to the economy, the God of Things, and will likely not get them back.

I will hopefully be able to rescue my grandson.

Be a guerilla thinker and anonymous writer so long as you are at the mercy of the economy. Your goal should be self-sufficiency like Jack Donovan and the Wolves of Vinland have pioneered, working in arts and trades away from the feminized workplace. Our economy is a cultural negation matrix. If you want to become a superior man and raise whole children treat the economy like kryptonite.

J comments:

Hi James-

I've been reading your articles on and off for about a year. Could you elaborate on what you meant by these lines, specifically 'temporary family':

"If you just make the money to keep a temporary family and then watch your children dispersed into the atomized world, like I have, you will find yourself standing at the edge of a yawning abyss. I surrendered my sons to the economy, the God of Things, and will likely not get them back.

I will hopefully be able to rescue my grandson."

Are you referring to making just enough vs generation wealth? Or to wealth for wealth sake versus a higher calling? Or something else?

My son is four and I have been blessed since his birth to achieve enough success through entrepreneurism/investing to have left the j.o.b. world behind (seemingly for good, unless something horrible happens). I think often on what his own path might be though, and whether it is possible to stimulate/help him into following that same path as a teenager, so that he can avoid the infinite forms of 'substitute masculinity' and 'substitute sacrality' that permeate our culture today- especially for young people (video games, porn, drugs, degeneracy, self-destruction, victimology, etc.). Yet on the other hand the danger of giving too much help rears its head and ending up with him 'r-selected', to use that terminology.

Thank you for the excellent sight and sharing your wisdom.

The author responds:

My thoughts on "temporary family" is that that is what a nuclear family has become under the modern system of debt slavery and real estate drift, in which neighborhoods are intentionally blighted to force suburban migration.

The nuclear family, alone, could be maintained as an extended family network under a non-predatory economic system, but tends to be scattered.

For instance my Uncle, a successful man, a millionaire, had five children. He and his wife live in Florida.

His son lives in Pittsburg with his wife and two sons.

His oldest daughter lives in Kansas with her husband, her children having scattered with the shifting career winds.

His next oldest daughter lives in Illinois, with four children, having been abandoned by her husband who moved to Boston.

His next to youngest daughter lives in Baltimore with two sons, her husband having abandoned her for drugs and alcohol.

His youngest lives in San Francisco with her husband and two sons.

How in Hell is Uncle Fred going to protect his family?

What are the chances he will be near in a crisis?

The combination of career drift and real estate blight acting on the nuclear family atomizes all but the strongest nuclear units and these are stretched tenuously.

Also, with the media machine what it is, it is highly unlikely that any given generation of a family will share the same values and outlook as their parents, which stresses individuals immeasurably.

Biblical Babes: Rebekah

Lynn & James Discuss Spouse Selection for Men

James, I don't know whether to call it ironic, but you often put me in the mood to pick up my trusty King James Version, the one my uncle gave me when I was seven years old, with a gilt edge and my name engraved in gold letters in the corner of the red leather cover, adorned with both a Cross and a Star of David. Sorry Jeremy, you can keep your NIV, the KJV is the only Bible for me.

Your readership seems to overlap with those of the seduction community (AKA pick-up artists) as well as those who advocate a return to patriarchy. In light of that, I thought it would be fun to seek your thoughts on some of the Bible's great love stories. Let's start with Abraham's son Isaac, and his niece Rebekah:

Genesis 24:15 - 25

And it came to pass, before he had done speaking, that, behold, Rebekah came out, who was born to Bethuel, son of Milcah, the wife of Nahor, Abraham's brother, with her pitcher upon her shoulder. And the damsel was very fair to look upon, a virgin, neither had any man known her: and she went down to the well, and filled her pitcher, and came up. And the servant ran to meet her, and said, Let me, I pray thee, drink a little water of thy pitcher. And she said, Drink, my lord: and she hasted, and let down her pitcher upon her hand, and gave him drink. And when she had done giving him drink, she said, I will draw water for thy camels also, until they have done drinking. And she hasted, and emptied her pitcher into the trough, and ran again unto the well to draw water, and drew for all his camels. And the man wondering at her held his peace, to wit whether the LORD had made his journey prosperous or not. And it came to pass, as the camels had done drinking, that the man took a golden earring of half a shekel weight, and two bracelets for her hands of ten shekels weight of gold; And said, Whose daughter art thou? tell me, I pray thee: is there room in thy father's house for us to lodge in? And she said unto him, I am the daughter of Bethuel the son of Milcah, which she bare unto Nahor. She said moreover unto him, We have both straw and provender enough, and room to lodge in.

My thoughts -- men like to see a woman willing to do work, particularly if it is to benefit his own comfort, a cool drink on a hot day, a tidy home, a well cooked meal. The idea of an arranged marriage is not totally abhorrent to me, especially now that I am a parent, but I truly believe there is a genetic predisposition to rebelliousness in Europeans that would prevent it from taking hold among our people. There may be cultural components among Asian and Subcontinental people that assists, but the DNA has a strong effect.

James, what are your thoughts?

-Lynn [Lynn's questions appear below in italics.]

How do you rate the camel-watering seduction technique?

Getting to know, or forming an opinion of another person's qualities in a work setting has resulted in some very stable relationships in the retail food business. Whether you are a man or a woman, seeing a potential mate engaged in their trade provides an authentic measure of their character, quite the opposite of "dating," which tends to be a waltz to the bottom of our beings in search of the lesser angels of our nature.

Would you trust your brother to find a wife for your son?

I would trust him to find a prospect, but never to make the actual purchase.

I am not even going to ask if you would trust your uncle to find a wife for you.

I would definitely trust my uncle to find a wife for me, even sealing the deal and making the buy. Our tastes in women are that much in alignment. I have brought a couple girlfriends to family functions were my Uncle Fred and Aunt Patsy were in attendance. When he hugged the more well-curved of the two he grinned and would not let her go until my aunt slapped his shoulder and said, "Fred, let the poor thing go!"

He then patted me on the back and asked, "Friend or sleepover friend."

"Sleepover," I answered and he patted me between the shoulder blades so hard it hurt and said, "You've turned into a good judge of women."

Have you given any thought to the despicable Semitic practice of cousin marriage? My Pakistani Sunni neighbors have confirmed to me that cousin marriage, or uncle-niece marriage is the norm there.

I have spent little wattage ruminating upon the breeding practices of that strain of humanity. I am more interested in how local varieties of humans have reproduced for good and ill. I do find it fascinating that the advent of Christendom, facilitated in some instances of conversion via the wives of kings, princes and chiefs to whom sissy holy men of the Christian orders were permitted access as they were not seen as a sexual threat, brought to European royalty the practice of cousin marriage. Many people do not realize, that by the eve of the Great War in 1914, that virtually the entire ruling class of the nations of

Europe were related by blood. This curious impulse to keep power within family blood lines by inbreeding has contributed to the degeneration of numerous nation states throughout history and finally brought about the ruination of all of Europe in the Two Acts of the War of European Suicide. It is also noteworthy that one develops inferior dogs from wolf stock by inbreeding. This fact leads me to believe that such cultural patterns serve the purpose of human domestication, though have no evidence for this at hand.

James, I thought about calling this series Biblical Bitches, but I can barely type the word out. You know I like to keep it G-rated, so Biblical Babes it is.

Thanks for your thoughts, James. You and your uncle are well prepared for the return of the patriarchy. I want to mention that cousin marriage, or the lack thereof, especially among the masses, is a point of interest in the alt-right, as it may have major behavioral consequences. Interested readers should look into the archives at https://hbdchick.wordpress.com/

Thanks, as always!

-Lynn

Lynn, the inbreeding among the Christian elite intensified over the ages as they became deracinated and secularized over time, with, at the advent of WWI, the elite possessed primarily of class consciousness, rather than racial identity or religious faith. Much of the intellectual opinion on the Right was very race conscious, but the people in power had drifted to the center. I suspect that there is a relationship here, especially in view of the fact that cousin marriage was not an indigenous European tradition, but an import adopted by the elite, who also drew their religious bearings from outside of Europe.

The WordPress link you provided is fascinating, and, I believe, depicts an Eastern European buffer zone, what Stoddard might have called a "dyke." It is simply fascinating that Western Europe is well on its way to undergoing a thorough transformation into a Middle Eastern Culture even as the East is resisting.

Biblical Babes: Regarding Rivka

(aka Rebekah)
by Baruch Kogan

Arranged marriage was common among European aristocrats until pretty recently.

Inbreeding is not deleterious in and of itself, except when it concentrates deleterious recessive traits. However, over time, these traits wash out. Advantageous recessive traits do not. Examples of successful sustained inbreeding in humans include the Egyptian Pharaohs. In other mammals, you have the naked mole rats, which are eusocial and where the queen breeds with her offspring, with no ill effect.

In any case, this is not totally relevant to us [Jews], because in our society, cousin marriage is combined with a steady inflow of converts.

For instance, the tribe of Judah is descended from Tamar, a Canaanite woman. Joseph married Asenath, a Egyptian noble girl, and the tribes of Ephraim and Menashe come from her. Moses married Tzipporah, who was either a Midianite or a Kushite. The Davidic dynasty comes from Ruth, a Moabite convert. Etc., etc.

Your Pakistanis are not Semitic but Aryan, by the way. Cousin marriage is also practiced in Iran, and has been from the time of the Ancient Persians, and is common among Hindus. So you might as well refer to it as a "despicable Aryan practice."

The mentality of Abraham, who sends Eliezer to find a wife for his son, is not "find him a hot wife." This is the normal thinking in a society of sexual anarchy, where people mate like wild dogs coming together, i.e., the modern West. You should not project it onto our patriarchs, who were completely different people living in a different time with a different mentality. In a normal, functional society, this is not how things are done. You look for a good family, if possible (Abraham didn't have this option,) and good character traits. When you put people together who are generally compatible, and their marriage is a fait accompli, they learn how to love each other with the years. Notice that when they were married, Isaac was 40. When a man marries late, he does not look for the same things that he does when he marries early, and in any case, Isaac was subject to his father's authority in all aspects (notice how his life was an almost complete parallel of Abraham's).

Baruch,

Thanks for your response, I was hoping you would chime in. I appreciate your comments on marriage in a more holistic patriarchal context.

I should have credited Moldbug for the inbreeding comment, but I was trying to draw you out and it worked. I am over 13% Ashkenazi myself, and grateful for the admixture, granted to me by my great-grandmother who was trafficked by fellow Jews to the remote tip of South America as a burlesque dancer and prostitute. Her village in Eastern Europe was later targeted for a pogrom, so I guess it worked out after all. August beginnings!

Pakistani Muslims tend to be either conquered Hindus of any caste, or else converted members of the lowest castes, seeking social equality as Muslims. I don't know what kind my neighbors might be, but the level of inbreeding is staggering. It takes a long time and a large population to wash out deleterious genes, the Pakistanis aren't there yet, obviously. Hindus are highly endogamous within their castes but not so much into cousin marriage, the rampant inbreeding among Pakistanis has to be the Muslim/Arab (hence Semitic) influence I think.

Thanks again, Baruch, hope to hear from you more

-Lynn

Biblical Babes: Rahab

James, for our second installment of Biblical Babes let's look at the story of Rahab.

In their bid to conquer the city of Jericho, the Israelites sent a pair of spies to the city, where they lodged with the harlot, Rahab.

I had to think for a while before I figured out that the subtext of this story is the mirror image of that in your Man Gearing series, especially in the short fictional piece *The Last Bar on Earth*. Rahab's city is about to be sacked by divine decree, and she seizes the opportunity to attach herself and her family to her new Hebrew overlords. Rahab wisely takes the feminine course of action. First, she praises the masculine feats of the Israelites and their God. Then she takes a risk on behalf of the spies and conceals them from her doomed king. Finally, she asks plainly for what she wants, the lives and property of her family preserved in the coming battle.

Joshua 6:9-13

And she said unto the men, I know that the LORD hath given you the land, and that your terror is fallen upon us, and that all the inhabitants of the land faint because of you. For we have heard how the LORD dried up the water of the Red sea for you, when ye came out of Egypt; and what ye did unto the two kings of the Amorites, that were on the other side Jordan, Sihon and Og, whom ye utterly destroyed. And as soon as we had heard these things, our hearts did melt, neither did there remain any more courage in any man, because of you: for the LORD your God, he is God in heaven above, and in earth beneath. Now therefore, I pray you, swear unto me by the LORD, since I have shewed you kindness, that ye will also shew kindness unto my father's house, and give me a true token: And that ye will save alive my father, and my mother, and my brethren, and my sisters, and all that they have, and deliver our lives from death.

James, this plan worked out for Rahab in the end. Rahab understood implicitly something that is really hard for us girls to accept here in the 21st century, that men are always in charge, one way or another, and your best bet is to use your feminine gifts to work within that frame to secure yourself and your family. Am I on the right track here, or is this another female derail of the man gearing focus?

-Lynn

Lynn, you made the correct point clearly and concisely.

Let's keep in mind that this hot little harlot also has the advantage of an accurate prophecy at her disposal. She knows who is going to win, when in reality, most girls do not know who is coming out on top and their own measures to secure their family's survival may be fraught with doubts.

Situations in heavily managed states and in post-collapse scenarios are going to be much harder to predict, which makes the woman's action in Rahab's position all the more important, as the issue is in doubt and her loyalty or betrayal may make the difference between the rise and fall of men.

This makes my favorite whore, Delilah, a more practical biblical example of female spies making a difference in a tribal setting.

Also, as I have often warned, men who plot against a powerful enemy or resist an evil state, that is, heroes, patriots, and also criminals, cannot let women into the decision circle and must not confide in their wives, for the women of the underdog, of the men with an obviously less than 50% chance of success, are natural traitors and can be expected to align themselves with the likely victor, not with their ties of blood or soil.

For this reason, men who might defend themselves and their own from anarcho-tyrannical proxy forces may not depend on or confide in women concerning their actions. Also note, that women do not generally support the obvious underdog [the real reason for the paucity of women on the AltRight], but rather the overlord.

'My Daughter'

One Civilized Man's Dilemma and One Barbarian's Solution

A lifelong friend of mine stopped through town on the way to a solitary week's vacation at the beach.

Things weighed heavily on his mind.

He and his wife work fulltime, and they own their house together outright, both in second careers.

His older daughter is a single mother living outside the house, but still incapable of supporting herself, as she depends on him and not the sperm donor for her sustenance.

The younger daughter, at age 17, is a high school dropout, who quit school at age 16 after being involved in a love affair with her 22-year-old female coach. This was technically statutory rape, but the parents remained supportive of the daughter's lifestyle choice.

The 24-year-old lesbian lover now lives in the family home in the daughter's bedroom, which bothers him, but apparently not his wife.

He is set on returning from the beach to give an ultimatum to these two lesbians sponging off of him, as neither the daughter nor lover work! The daughter did work for a while—the lesbian coach, never.

I advised: "Bro, if I had a 24-year-old woman under my roof, not working, not related to me, she'd be putting out for the patriarchy."

He said, "But she's a lesbian."

I admonished, "They can be turned. It's just like retraining a janitor to be a stock clerk—the same tools, just different applications."

He rejoined, "Somehow I think The Wife might not be onboard with the idea."

We both sighed and spoke of simpler times.

*****

When I returned to the Slave Girl's den and told her of this, she said, "He should tell her to butch up like a man and get a job!"

She then hesitated and asked, "You didn't offer to go back home and straighten that lesbian out, did you?"

With a Clintonian twinkle in my mind's eye, I parsed, "I took the higher road."

She crawled closer, "I'm so glad I've read about Big Ron's fuck parade. I was beginning to think you were a real womanizer until I read about him!"

She then continued, adorably transparent in her line of inquiry, "Baby, are you still going to get together with Big Ron after you're done interviewing him?"

"Sure, he's a great guy."

*****

Later, as she is trimming my beard and shaving my head, she inquires poutingly, "Baby, will you go to strip bars with Big Ron?"

"I'm too old for that," I dodged.

"Baby," as the razor slides by my ear, "you never had sex with the strippers when you went to those places, did you?"

"Look," I scowled, "I passed those opportunities up back when I was fit enough to enjoy it. I'm not that guy that goes to a strip club and has sex with strippers."

She burst out, "But Big Ron's that guy!"

"Yes, Big Ron's that guy."

Seemingly contented, she sighed, "You know, I never thought I'd ever think of you as a good guy! Thank God for Big Ron. And look at you with that head shaved—you look so handsome."

"Thanks, Babe. Look, I know we had plans. But I'm going to head over to Hooters for a bite to eat."

"What?" she chirped with doubt dancing in her eyes.

"I'm short—you think you could give me twenty bucks, I'd hate to be a light tipper?"

Instead of going at me with the scissors in hand, she laughed in a ringing way, and I judged it safe to pass out in her bed, wishing my lifelong friend my silent best.

Amping Up the Race Hate

Two Minutes on a Diner Parking Lot with a Black Woman

Shawn, a black woman in her early 40s, had just bought me breakfast at a Baltimore County diner. This was the morning of Thursday, June 15, 2017. I had just finished interviewing her about some white fellows in her youth being rude, one by spitting at her feet another by calling her "nigger-nigger." She told me that this never deterred her from socializing with white men rather than blacks, as she dislikes the behavior of most black men and regards white men as the correct masculine standard.

As we stepped outside, a black man in a working pickup truck gave us both hateful looks, shook his head and drove off.

Earlier, in the diner, there had been a group of three white men, each about 30 years old, bearded, wearing baseball-style caps with the blacked out American flag on them and glaring at us, even talking about us in hushed tones. The men were all fit-looking though not athletic. One was my size, the other two were larger.

They walked down the ramp ahead of us, twice glancing back.

They walked to the right toward their vehicles and we followed, our vehicle being halfway from the door to their parking spots.

We stopped for a moment to savor the hate of the black man and Shawn quipped under her breath, "Nigga please, like I'd rather be with you than a white man."

We chuckled over that as we walked on.

As it turns out only two of the men—the two big ones—were parked down the lot. As those two said farewell to the shorter one and entered their pickup trucks he turned around and walked toward us.

Shawn tensed next to me as he glared at her, as if he were some sorcerer attempting to melt her mind.

I switched my laptop case into my left hand and slid my right hand under my t-shirt to rest on the paracord tang of my skinning knife.

As he and I reached five paces from each other, her on my right and him on my left, he looked at my right hand, looked up into my eyes, swallowed, and nodded as if in respect.

At four paces, I grinned widely as she sucked in her breath next to me.

At three paces, as his feet stutter-stepped slightly and his eyes batted spastically, I said, "Hey."

At two paces, he bit his lip and looked bug-eyed at my grinning face as I smirked, "How's it goin'?"

His voice caught in his throat as his eyes bugged out and I placed my right hand across her back and we passed.

Shawn was aghast, "You were messing with him—trying to start something!"

"No, Girl," I said, "I could have kissed his wife and he wouldn't have gone there. All of his confidence is already driving off in their trucks."

"I can't believe you—OMG, you tried to start a fight over me!"

"I don't fight, Girl—I just thought he was all cute and cuddly looking and thought I'd let him know how much I appreciated his jealousy."

"Okay, you're crazy—and that was kind of fun."

"It was nothing but spontaneous man love, and you ruined it Baby Girl."

In my younger days, this happened to me often, whether I was with a black girl or a white girl or the insane Puerto Rican bitch. I was once the only person at an all black park with the best looking black girl on my arm. Only one negro wanted to fight over that and I gave him the same treatment. Packs of white boys were always tougher to deal with, even groups of cops would threaten me or try to make conversation with my girl as an intimidation tactic. The last time this happened to me was 2012 in Rosedale, in front of the Mars Supermarket, when three white dudes in a pickup tried to pick a fight with me when I was out with Megan.

I know what this is, have experienced it from the other side.

On three different occasions as a young man, between 1981-83, while I was married, I was drinking with friends—on one occasion camping—when one or more of them suggested beating up a man and raping his woman. In all cases these were spontaneous suggestions triggered by seeing a man with an attractive woman. These were all white couples that my friends expressed an urge to terrify and inseminate. I have heard military men brag about gang raping allied women in France and Vietnam. I have known a dozen women who were raped and gang raped, mostly by men of their own race.

As a tribalist, I need to be clear that this is the ugliest aspect of the tribal human mind and has largely been responsible for people allowing governments to usurp our former right to self-defense. Men of all three races I have been in contact with have expressed this desire to attack a couple and rape the woman, usually with me as part of the target couple.

I doubt very much if these three bearded white rabbits were of that mindset. I gathered that they simply disapproved of what they saw as my mating choice. This always brings out the worst in me. By myself I take the lowest friction route away from contact, but while with a woman my mind immediately turns to combat, not fighting, not defending, but stabbing, ripping, smashing and jump stomping.

This is how we are wired.

I am a tribalist with no tribe, the hand of very man against me, the hearts of my own race filled with hate for my failure to join in their seething blindness, an enemy of The State, for my refusal to condemn that same race, a tiny enemy of all the vast world and if I had a torch that would burn this planet to a cinder, I would light it.

This is who I am, a being suppressed by the artifice of being a father. If I had no sons I would have no other goal than snuffing out as many of the seething apes that defile this garden sphere as possible. But I have been seduced by simple biology into being one of you, so you are safe.

The Slave Girl

Surviving the Girl Cave: June 7, 2017

As I hobbled out of my jeans on a sprained ankle, one knee popping and my hand failing to open, I looked down at my slave girl there, admiring her form and saying so, indicating my approval of her attire, to which she reminded me there was none.

The patriarchal bestowal of favor still untaken, I indicated that one would have thought, having acquired a slave girl of such extreme proportions off the used block at the Robert E. Howard Memorial Slave Girl Collectors Convention, that one would expect more signs of hard use. Despite recently being forced to watch Black Dynamite and being made to memorize, "You can either hit the sheets or hit the streets," and being conditioned to respond positively to, "Bitch, nah," a streak of the petulant free woman remained, as evidenced by her reminder that slave girls, properly preserved through pampering, retain their value, and that one is much more apt to purchase a gladiator with some miles on him that almost immediately breaks down after taking him for his first test ride, than one is to be disappointed by a slave girl.

Thence, her scintillant eyes glinting with the fire of the female who feels herself ascendant and gaining power over her fading master, she simpered, "Baby, are you still going to show me how to use the sword?" nodding at the claymore, which I had placed over her headboard to commemorate her taking.

"Of course," I intoned, making a mental note to keep postponing the event.

Then she nodded at the combat knife she had purchased for my protection—which is illegal in so many ways I left it on her headboard rather than risk being taken into custody over carrying it—and asked, "Baby, from reading so much of your combat arts erudition, I understand that the knife is really the best defensive weapon. Will you show me how to use that?"

"Bitch, nah."

"Why?'

"Get me a beer—a shot of whiskey too."

After dutifully serving, she pressed for an answer, "Why not the knife, Baby?"

"Because it's a little too effective at close quarters for my comfort—okay?"

Some ways down that whiskey river I woke up, sure I was alive by the pain in my head, got dressed, grabbed the T-Cane and pack and headed out into the Harm County night, she watching me go like an earthling viewing an alien liftoff, from behind this bath towel bra that seemed a washcloth.

When I got to work and punched in, I checked my phone and saw this text, from Wed, Jun, 7 11:22:

"Just knocked over your carefully constructed bitch booby trap that you built on your side of the bed [with empty beer bottles] to keep bitches from coming up on you by surprise..."

Yes, there is more than one way to enforce patriarchal norms.

You young bucks out there, take note that the beer bottle palisade should be constructed 12-18 inches from the bed, works best on tile or hard wood, that you should maintain low lighting on that side and do not let your tactile senses slacken in case a suddenly unruly wench decides to creep up on you across the very field of her recent conquest.

My Family, My Enemy

Matriarchy: The Source of Defiance

The human being, as disgusting as it is, is an amazing ape.

I regard the Old Testament as history rather than the word of God, primarily because God is said to have made man in his own image.

I desire a better God than that.

My God is the center of the Universe, not a hairy patriarch on a throne of pillared cloud.

I further see the Old Testament as the seat of emasculation, the seed of the downfall of us all, with its focus on domestication and the sacred obsession with denaturing mankind and despoiling his habitat. In my defiant brain, the patriarchy of garden and house under a shepherd God is but a stepping stone out of—and necessarily back into—matriarchy.

Yesterday, in honor of Big Ron, I did a social experiment.

My estranged wife, with whom I remain on good terms and who reads this site just to see how much trouble I'm getting into, was visiting my mother while I was there. They are nearly next door neighbors.

My darling mother inquired as to why I would not be visiting next week and I told her I had a lot of proofing and editing to do. She waxed supportive, reminding me that she is a good proof reader, but that my content is so vile and my style so poor that she cannot bear to read my work.

She is in a painful position. Her son knows more about the world than any four people in her life and yet insists on criticizing it rather than making money off of it. She is worried about the blooming race war, about my dangerous living and is very concerned about the increasing hatred and intolerance in the media, but still wishes we could all just get along.

The woman next to her, who over a decade ago inexplicably kicked me out of the house I rented just because I was banging a few other chicks, mentioned that I am interviewing some interesting people and that she is a big Big Ron fan. I take the conversational ball and run with it, telling a few sexy pizza delivery and brutal fight tales from Big Ron's life. As I describe Big Ron biting the negro thumb on the trigger of the gun right around the corner from her Aunt Alice's old house in Hamilton, my mother rose, tiny and Elizabethan in her seat and said, "What kind of animal is this you are talking to?"

Faye broke in and said, "The kind of animal Mamma Faye would like to get to know—but your son won't let me meet him."

I retorted, "He's recovering from a bad back injury and you wrecked my spine in Ninety-Two. The last thing he needs is a romp with you."

My mother looked at her daughter-in-law aghast, as if to say, *Didn't you learn anything about the pitfalls of associating with such men by being married to my son?* [My mother, upon meeting one fine slave girl, was stricken with guilt and looked at me and pleaded, "Please don't hurt her—the poor thing is in love with you!"]

Faye shrugged her shoulder with a comic grin and I cut in, "Look, Ma, he's a real nice guy and if you didn't know his hobbies included beating up negroes and banging sluts, you'd find him quite personable. More importantly, if only a third of the men in Baltimore my age, had been like Big Ron, Baltimore would still be a place you could go play bingo and get a bite to eat."

She then raised her eyebrows and laughed, "That's certainly true. They never did touch your Uncle Bill."

In the end, the fact that not a soul in my fairly large family [except those like Uncle Bill who married in and have since passed away] believes that a man should stand and fight for his property, his space, his woman or his race, or anything else he might value, cherish or believe in, but tuck tail and run, while it remains the chasm that divides me from my entire biological line, provided the very spark for my rebellion against the sissy system that had weaned me to revel in victimhood and wallow in alienated despair. The very sheep-eyed bowing of the head to those above and the rabbit-footed flight from those below that characterized my parents, my peers and those who have spawned limp-wristed and cotton-tailed since, is what awkwardly made me a man, someone worthy of being hated by those who they cowardly so fear.

In the end, as much as I disagree with their every morality and every sissy submission, I can thank my family for making me into a fighting man through their vapid resignation under the ominous weight of this evil nation.

That said, the poor old girl cried when I told her they ripped the Confederate monuments out in the night. She pined, "But we are supposed to have freedom of expression?"

I patted her on the hand and said, "It was a lie, Mom, a bright shining lie that I never believed for a minute."

She tried not to cry anymore as the monster she long ago brought into her neatly ordered world smiled and walked away.

The Way Forward

Pondering Masculine Extinction

This weekend my youngest son told me he would not be having children. He is a man who sticks to his plans and is loyal to the women in his life to a degree I find unfathomable. So, since that nice girl he married doesn't want kids, he won't have them.

That is that.

My oldest son is adopted, so my name will survive and hopefully my grandson will read something I've written, for I know his father and uncle will not.

This leaves me with a choice if I wish not to become entirely extinct.

Do I write and hope that something of my life experience will echo in an as yet unborn mind?

Or, do I father more children?

Fathering children in this nation of evil witches is something that would take enough financial assets that I would have to take my work out of publication, cease writing and recant about 2 million words of dissidence. This would enable me to find an Eastern European wife and house her in traditional style.

Ugh, I am so weary of women and their time-eating triviality that I think I shall stay the course as a writer.

But how I write will have to change since the Unite-the-Right assholes shit the bed for all dissenting white men and wound up the clock to four minutes to midnight for free thinking apes of the pale kind.

That is the subject for a piece on contingency writing, which is outside the scope of masculinity.

The Vile Root: Invalidation

Masculine Negation and the Mental Health of the Man

In seeking masculine companionship, or in accepting non-intimate relations with a woman[1] the man and his fellow, as with the hero and his fellow-fighter or the hero and the shaman, seek a purely spiritual bond that is forged in the face of a commonly understood pursuit.

In the case of two men fighting an enemy together, we have the simplest example.

[1] Cultures with habitually poor martial legacies and weak sissy men prohibit platonic friendship between men and women. I believe this is done for the purpose of domesticating the mind, of depriving the man or youth of healthy, no strings attached admiration. This hero-cultivating relationship was provided to a limited degree [it can never by widespread, really] via the tradition of unconsummated courtly love, in the High Middle Ages in which a knight would fight purely for a single woman's admiration. This was a later stylistic remnant of something that had existed earlier in The West, was probably always thin on the ground and is currently extinct.

Then there is the case of the young fighter going into the ring where the old fighter has been before.

Thirdly, there is the rare case of the female observer who actually understands the trials the man is facing and appreciates his efforts on her behalf, on behalf of the company, the tribe, the race, the nation, or simply on the behalf of any person who succeeds through suffering. Nursing in modern warfare is a surviving niche for this ancient impulse.

Modernity is an advanced state of technological civilization in which man is thrice removed from the trials of life: he does not seek, does not hunt, does not fight, but engages in tasks previously reserved for women and is now at their spiritual mercy. Modernity therefore favors the feminine holistically, with an all-encompassing drive to feminize the male.

The Vile Root is an ongoing exploration of masculine negation offered as a resource to the reader of the *Masculine Axis*. Men have often claimed that it was they who built civilization and that women are their cultivated version of a wild seed. It is not so. *Some* men have duplicitously engineered civilization to domesticate *most* men, using women alternately as hostages and purveyors of the system.

The primary tool a woman uses to domesticate, neuter, denature, emasculate a man, is a tactic called invalidation. Invalidation is the means by which womankind engage in the spiritual mutilation of their children, their men and their fellow women. Women are so addicted to the mechanics of impulsive invalidation that they continuously mutilate themselves in their own mind's eye. Most women that employ invalidation techniques to hollow and then crush the persons in their life circle do not even realize what they do and cannot qualify the process.

As a teenager, my friends and I noticed that as soon as a youth began dating woman he left the group, ignored all of his old friends and wed himself to her, keeping her exclusive company. He stopped playing contact sports, stopped taking all risks, cared no more for the approval of his mates other than the jealousy of virgins for his mated status. This is less so now than it was in my youth, largely because society in general has taken up the woman's divisive whip. One may now be emasculated by a woman you do not know—by some bitch on TV, by some feminized sissy in the locker room at the YMCA, by a coworker.

It is enough to state that in terms of the larger society the civilized woman has only three purposes:

1. To bring forth young,
2. To invalidate those tiny souls so that they will become self-policing gears in the social engine, and
3. To invalidate those men and aspiring-men in their own mind's eye, to snatch away the life of a race by blowing out the heroic flame in a man's soul and planting in its stead the vile

> root of self-doubt that shall curse him in his every endeavor.

It is important to remember that even if you consider yourself a civilized man and a defender of civilization, that civilization itself yearns for your destruction, has a driving thirst to evaporate your masculine identity. All that is necessary for a civilization to fall is for it to succeed in denaturing its men; for the men who protect civilization to permit its weak, its meek, its simpering, its seductive to drain them of their barbaric impulses; for the irony of every civilization is that it can only stand up against itself and its assailants through the intercession of barbarian hands. A civilization rises on the shoulders of the very men it rejects and then crumbles in their absence.

Rob Jones comments:

This is tripe. It is all assertions and not facts. The conclusions are forwarded as truth and come across as if writer expects they are beyond reproach.

The author responds:

This is my premise for the theory, for which I will present anecdotes as examples to advance the theory, which is based primarily on experience, particularly my experience coaching and advising young men, who have been negatively impacted by this behavior, as well as my own lifetime of experiences with invalidation such as: "only black men can box" and "the only path to success is a university education," etc.

I use this site to build books from front to back. The advancing of critical comments such as yours are important to the process. For instance, it is obvious to me now, after reading your comment, that I should have given a brief narration of my experience with this process as an introduction.

Here is one common example, which happened to me last night, when a coworker said, "Oh, you don't have much to do tonight." I, in fact, had the heaviest order on the crew. His comment was meant to strike at my confidence, to keep me on the defensive so I would not notice that he had the light load of the night, a fact that means nothing to me. This is a type of "projection" I suppose and makes the early going for new employees very trying.

This is said, in the business I work in [retail food], constantly by some coworkers to others in order to instill in them a sense that they don't measure up. Having worked in 34 supermarkets over four decades, I have noted this as a dominant behavior common to all companies, in all departments and from top to bottom, in both union and non-union stores.

I have long noticed that men who come to me for boxing instruction have suffered much of this type of discouragement from mothers and others in their life. Overcoming this third-person negativity is often the boxing trainer's greatest hurdle.

I would recommend, as a source, a small red book, published towards the end of the last century, titled *Nasty People*.

Thanks, Rob.

Rob Jones responds:

Thanks for taking the time to respond. I was sent to your article from Gab.com. Anyway, I get where you're coming from but I happen to believe it is the maneuvering for dominance, like in the incident you mention in your response, that makes men who and what they are. We are meant to dominate and control. And we need to learn and develop these skills. History shows us what happens when women take over, everything falls apart. With a few exceptions this is not only the norm but the rule. It can be seen clearly in society today, women are quickly replacing men in the work force in places they don't have the skills or intelligence to be and things are collapsing. Hence their need to bring in the Muslims–they need alphas to come back into society and put them in their place and the milquetoast beta males (who got that way being raised exclusively by mothers) that are already here aren't up to the task. Now I can say all of this stuff but none of it means anything because I can't demonstrate the truth of any of it, I just happen to believe it is true. For a thesis to have any validity at all it has to be sent into the sphere of objectivity and tested with the scientific method meaning pulled apart and re-constructed with evidence (not interpretation). Otherwise it comes off, in my case, as hate speech.

The author responds:

Rob, thanks for the well-reasoned response.

I absolutely agree that the maneuver for dominance is what makes us men and may even be what we are.

I see the female form of pecking order aggression as toxic to the male, particularly the boy. I think this is why traditional societies remove the boy from the women's sphere when he begins to develop physically.

The invalidation concept–the way I am looking at it–has to do with the support element of the society negating the individual. For instance, I think we can agree that getting punched in the face is an important rite of passage for a man, however a mother publicly punching out her son while calling him a "bitch-ass nigga" [which happened and was applauded during the Baltimore Riots] is going to retard, distort and/or twist his development, and has been the very mechanism which has hampered so many young men in that community from developing a balanced approach to aggression.

To use football as an example, the players on the other team should knock the snot out of you and test you, maybe even snarl stuff about your mother to test your discipline. But for the water boy or cheer leaders to insult, mock and even strike their own player is a negative interaction, which, if done at the wrong time, can harm the young man's development by twisting him.

I am not an alpha male and have spent much of my life helping them succeed from a fringe position. I see much modern dysfunction, from TV comedy to feminism, as a way to retard the development of the all-important alpha male. The only masculine type that gains power from invalidation is the fringe taboo type or psychopath–which I call the Omega–who feed on it. These types can be valuable tools for the alpha

[Enkidu was the taboo counterpart-sidekick to Gilgamesh, the alpha male], but if your society starts having them as its heroes [Jason Bourne, the Man with no Name, Vampires, Werewolves, etc.,] rather than heroizing the alpha male, that is a society in trouble. A healthy society has Wyatt Earp, not Doc Holiday as its hero, Daniel Boone, not Mingo, the Lone Ranger not Tonto...

Thanks again, Rob.

Her Daughter

The Vile Root: Invalidation for Older Men

For a society to scrub cultural residue from whatever tribal skin it has not yet shed, its men of middle age and older must be brought low, must lack the confidence in their opinions and withhold them from the young. The best way to achieve this is to develop scorn for adult men by the young. Most commercials since 1980 have been devoted to depicting the knowledgeable class of men—men who have survived beyond age 35—as fools. This has recently switched racial gears. In my youth older black men were forever depicted as fools. Now it is white men who are the TV fools of make believe.

For you older fellows below is an accumulation of examples from my personal life:

I began dating women that were my age and a few years older when I hit age 40. Most of these women had children that were teens or young adults. Without fail, after meeting their children, these women at some later time, out of the blue, when I was feeling confident and friendly and open, would just say "My daughter can't stand you!"

They always said it out of context.

They always said it with a wicked, bratty grin.

They always said it for effect, to hurt me.

For me, the effect was distancing. It let me see the bitch for the witch that she was, let me now that she sought my ultimate spiritual demise, and put me on my guard. I am an alienated "Omega" or "Taboo" type of man. I thrive on solitude. Insults only make me wince and send me to my place of inner solitude.

For Beta males, or "followers" and for Alpha males or "leaders" the effects can be more toxic as they are more conditioned to human approval. That is why I believe strongly that any man who places a high value on human approval should immediately break contact with any woman who says such things to him and that he spend time in a masculine fraternity, a gym, a gun club, a karate school or biker club. If you try to change this bitch it will bring out the bitch in you. Don't do it. If she is fun in the sack, keep her for that and ignore the barbs, never placing value on her opinion.

As with most female invalidation tactics, if she knows what she is doing, she probably construes it as a method to keep you close to her. By pointing out that younger women are not attracted to you, she feels assured that you will settle for her. For, according to the invalidation methods used by commercial society to convince her that she instantly became hideous at 35, she can't compete with a younger face.

If your lady friend tells you how bad her daughters think you are, then you should dump her and then fuck one of her daughters—ideally both at the same time—for this would have the exact same effect on her spirit as her words were intended to have on yours. However, as a practical matter, she was probably right about her daughter. You see, adult women try to rule their mothers according to these negative invalidation tactics. If they see she is happy with a strong man, she will be less easy to brow beat into loans and baby-sitting. So they will accuse Mom of dating a bad man, or of lettering her pussy get in the way of her feminist ethics. So, in light of this probability, her daughter does not deserve your attention, so settle for banging a nice waitress working her way through college.

Keep in mind throughout this series that most women have little or no agency and are simply foisting the pain onto you that others have dumped on them. In a very practical sense it is not worth hurting her feelings and seeking to do so simply puts you on her inferior, feminine moral plane. Don't be a spiteful bitch. Wish her a nice day and go on your way.

Whew!

On False Validation Among Men

Some time ago I arranged for sparring at a martial arts school that taught the skill set of stick-fighting for one of my stick-fighters. I was injured and unable to spar. When we walked through the door and saw a small army of muscular studs, beef, beef and leaner beef, I felt certain that he would get plenty of work and also be able to bring some of these full contact MMA guys—but non-contact stick-fighters—into the Bone Bruising Brotherhood of extension weapon knuckle-headery.

Our on-site contact, the guy that trained and sparred with us from this school, had spoken to them and they were supposedly stoked. The school owner, who I have known for many years, was glad to see us, really hoping these muscular, manly men would explore the contact application of the system he teaches.

My man was nervous. All of these guys were bigger and more muscular and he was supposed to spar with them all. I said, "Relax, they are raw, just work with them, make friends, nobody gets hurt."

Taking one look at my fighter coolly unpacking his gear, this crew of studs who had been doing some sparring with our on-site guy rushed as one to get their gear and leave—a veritable herd of frightened steers filing out the door before my man could even get his cup and gloves on.

The same fighter met me at another school at another time to spar with a towering tattooed stud who nervously greeted him. This guy had seen Chuck spar and complimented him. Chuck said, "Nobody gets hurt—we're all on the same learning curve helping each other along."

This did not allay his obvious dread of a stick on flesh encounter, even at tapping velocity. Seeing this, a longtime, non-contact stick spinner, who has never sparred, interceded and bailed his friend out, "Oh, this is for advanced students. I'll let you know when you're ready. Not yet, you don't want to get hurt."

Both the men politely drifted away from Chuck, then he overheard them in the dressing room, one saying, "Whew, brother, thanks for bailing me out of that—I'm not ready for that level of brutality."

You would think these men are speaking of boxing with a savage pro who liked hurting people or wrestling with a dire wolf. But this "brutality" they speak of is simple tactical sparring. Slow pace, "let me know if I tap you too hard," practice with head piece and gloves and elbow pads. This format has been engaged in by people from seven to seventy, 70 pounds to 410 pounds, without serious injury. But, in Sissy America, the thought of contact training with a seasoned fighter is regarded with the dread of a North Korean missile launch, with man after man willing to offer false validation, feminine comfort in manly guise, for the multitude of posing cowards among us who wish to wear manhood on a sleeve, a patch, a badge, a belt, while their so-called "brothers" assist them in the delusion that they are men in spirit as well, when they are not, but rather women writhing within a male structure.

The zero risk feminine culture of supporting the inaction and weakness implicit in modern life has spirituality maimed generations of men and turned them into drones. Such false validation of cowardice is advanced in terms of artistic purity and sensible training in most martial arts schools, schools which can only pay their bills if middle-class, single mothers feel like it is an appropriate child day care center.

The rot is nearly complete, even infecting MMA students and turning boxing gyms into nearly empty equipment lockers.

While invalidation of a man by women and seniors in a cultural support position is a corrosive aspect of modernity—eroding masculinity from cradle to grave—the sissy act of validating self-limiting fears of the kind exemplified above is just as dangerous as feminine emasculation, but taken together they conspire to unman most of male-kind.

Adam Swinder comments:

It just blows my mind when I hear or read about MMA fighters avoiding contact with weapons. If a fat everyman like me can train and compete for 10 years, what's stopping these muscleheads from doing the same? It's really not that big a deal, weapon sparring. It's fun! And the intensity you were offering is the kind that I can do (and have done) with most women, and leave them uninjured and better informed about contact.

The author responds:

Of course, Adam, we know it's not the physical fear. These are guys that sweated a lot to gain a skill set that offers status. Remember, that most MMA "fighters" will not spar with just their hands and will not get in the ring with a boxer, even for practice, unless they can kick–and then they refuse a second round.

The weapon fear is all about protecting the ego. The boxing fear is physical and mental. MMA guys will roll all day long with world class BJJ men, but they will not spar with a local boxer unless the rules of engagement permit them to work outside of his skill set. This same fear exists with MMA guys regarding collegiate and Olympic wrestlers. When Team Ground Control was first formed as the Baltimore BJJ Club one of their original members was the assistant wrestling coach at Curly, where you went to school and I coached weapons and boxing. I think his name was Esau and he had been on the Iranian Olympic Team! John Erwin told me that when they used to line up to practice take downs and throws that all these buff BJJ guys would be in line praying, "Oh my God" until they had to step up to this guy and get thrown like a rag doll. Of course, John was nuts so he enjoyed it like riding a roller coaster and was also willing to box with boxers.

Beyond Unthinking Ego

Notes on Baseball and Character Selection

On the Tuesday night of July 18, 2017, I found myself outlining articles while watching the Baltimore Orioles play the Texas Rangers. A casual view of the game and the conduct of the players, compared to the flamboyant, criminal childishness of football and basketball stars, brought to mind a conversation had the month before with Kevin Michael Grace, concerning the relative maturity and decency of major league baseball players compared to NFL and NBA players. Kevin pointed out to me that this is related to the fact that baseball players rarely start at the top level when first drafted, being relegated to honing their craft in the minor league ranks, where football and basketball standouts are thrown into competition more quickly.

What might be the specific reasons for this being the case?

Throughout most of my life, I have viewed sports beyond combat in the ancient way, as games, pastimes, not serious activities. However, that narrow view fails to take into account the huge influence sports have as public diversions and their value as reflections upon these elements of society which remain stable, improve, or most likely, decay and fall away.

I viewed this game and three interviews with players with an eye towards making an initial assessment of the qualities required of the players by their sport, which might generalize to social and combat function.

Most striking was the comment by home run hitter Tray Mancini that, "A lot of runs are thrown, not hit," an egoless assignment of his homerun to a miscalculation on his opponent's part, a type of admission many postmodern athletes are incapable of making. Since I played baseball and football for two seasons each and followed both with equal infrequency as a spectator, I was acutely aware that football is a game of industrial level over specialization, with few players capable of functioning outside their specialty, none operating both offensively and defensively, and most not engaging in the more demanding half of the hunter complex.

Every sport I have surveyed includes the two fundamental aspects of the hunt: aiming and chasing, aiming requiring more forethought, precision and consideration. By this standard, football is a nearly retarded game in terms of its relationship to the hunt. Whereas every basketball player must aim and run, only a tiny minority of football players engage in aiming, these being the quarterback and kickers.

Therefore, on a primal level, football fails to simulate the hunt, which was the setting in which our kind learned to function cooperatively toward goal attainment.

In baseball, despite its specialization, every player—except for the pitcher in the American League and the designated hitter, both positions being corruptions of the game to excite the idiot masses—is expected to operate both offensively and defensively, another aspect in which American Football fails in comparison to simpler sports such as basketball.

However, the two aspects of baseball that are most unique are virtually absent from other major league sports: its leisurely pace and interactive aiming are unique to the sport in the modern spectrum. The focus of the game is the duel between the pitcher throwing and the batter batting. Having once had an opportunity to try and bat against a major league pitcher, I understand that one must have a special level of reaction time and visual motion acuity to be able to track a ball thrown at that speed. I recall vividly still seeing the ball leave Randy's hand as it sizzled by me unseen.

This duel of patience and calculated delivery, engaged in sporadically by each player, and the agrarian pace of the competition, echoes the circumstances of life for those who conquered America. The crux of the most popular sport of the 19th century and of America for most of the 20th Century is a test of patience, timing and execution.

During the formative years of American baseball, roughly from the Civil War to WWII, America was, more than any other nation, a land of the long gun, of riflemen in uniform and on the ritual hunt for ungulates on the hoof. These two conditions, perhaps an echo of the other earlier age [with most American players drawn from outside of major cities], cultivates more socially-sustainable athletes than the celebrity survivors of the pseudo-combat sport of football.

In terms of measuring the physiques of the athletes, more attain the balanced Pentathlete form that Aristotle implied was best than the other sports mentioned. Also, just as I have noticed a higher level of intelligence among stick fighters than boxers, the top batters and the pitchers I saw interviewed—Tray Mancini, Chris Davis and Dylan Bundy—demonstrated hyperactive binocular eye movement. Watch interviews of top hitter and pitchers and note the open, mobile, triangulating eyes, as if the active eye movement of a wolf were combined with the intense binocular vision of a leopard or lion.

In a functional way, I am of the opinion that baseball is our psychologically eldest sport, accounting for it being among the most politely conducted and impulse-controlled sports that involve running, accounted for by its intense focus on aiming under stress. In baseball, every player is a quarterback and is required to attain an older, less command-oriented psychology than the sport that has overtaken it in the

American mind's eye, football, exemplified by the criminal goons of the National Felony League.

Combative Appropriation

Among the Men of the Hanged God, Out of Service, PA, July 22 & 23, 2017

As the only heathen to make it to Out Of Service, Pennsylvania to fight in the well-watered hollow of a mountain, I had a few consolation prizes for letting down our Christian allies by not fielding an effective opposition:

For the second year in a row I brought the thunder of the old gods to their sunny day as we fought and sparred in the drenching rain.

I came out on top of a truly sick knife duel with Nero the Pict, with whom I spent three nights drinking and exchanging experiences had among the ruins of Baltimore.

Dennis the jock beat me thrice with the stick and shield, of which I used to be the best practitioner. This means that I'm not the end of a line but a progress marker.

Their chief, Sean beat me decisively in our every engagement, including a long round of boxing sparring. I did my faded best, but as a coach, the worst outcome would have been to beat him and he proved to have learned every lesson he should have extracted from our fight 14 months ago.

Ulric Kerensky boxed competitively for almost three full rounds against the squatish, heavy-footed Pict, marking a huge stride for the young genius into the world of physical aggression. Ulric also informed me that "your reader from Syracuse sends his regards," a compliment which felt all the better for being anonymous.

Keith, a young Christian who survived the Detroit race wars of the 1990s without succumbing to hate, put on the gloves and fought until his body cramped up, and fought again, more positive about becoming a more muscular Christian after his bouts than before.

Most of all, for me, for my shade, the one thing I created with another gone man, Chuck Goetz, Modern Agonistics, a blatantly pagan slobber-knocker ritual, is being kept alive in a better place than Baltimore, where it has died along with most good things. All who participated kept the contact level at a mutually accessible place on the learning curve, so no man got reduced, but all gained. In the future, contact will amp up as the skill and experience level rises. For now the goals of masculine elevation for all were met.

Combat arts are about nurturing a masculine rite that might keep souls from falling into dust even while the body lives, in those inevitably emasculating future times, and, like the art of boxing being passed from race to race and back again, being preserved by ancients in stone and script to be resurrected by men of another bloodline, marks, in my heathen heart, the true universalist value, combativeness, without which we are all the sheep of cruel, earthly shepherds.

Thank you men, all five of you, for injecting some meaning into this weary year.

I would also like to thank Lili Hun for keeping the site going while I was away, Lynn Lockhart for generating extra BlogSpot posts and the Australian writing group working with Lili to compensate for the low output running up to the third Annual Man Weekend.

James, Monday, July 24 2017

'From the Day of My Death'

A Heroic View of Slavery

"I declare and ordain as free and quit of every obligation of captivity, subjection, and slavery, my captured slave Enrique, mulatto, native of the city of Malacca, of the age of twenty-six years more or less, that from the day of my death thenceforward forever the said Enrique may be free and manumitted, and quit, exempt, and relieved of every obligation of slavery and subjection, and that he may act as he desires and thinks fit."
-Ferdinand Magellan, June 19, 1519

Magellan also willed Enrique 1,000 maravedis.

The heroic view of slavery, expressed by Magellan in the will above, occupies the moral ground halfway between the primitive view of slavery encountered among Eastern Woodland Indians, who typically used slavery of militarily able men and boys as a trial period between capture and adoption, and the idea of plantation chattel.

In societies where warrior culture is important, total masculine reduction and invalidation of the owned person is not common. Even in a massive chattel society like Rome, since there was high value placed on martial spirit, slaves who made the warrior grade could be permitted to live on and serve as gladiators and bodyguards rather than simply be degraded like the chattel of the Early Modern Age. Even in savage Morocco, slaves such as Thomas Pellow might be elevated to warrior status and even command.

But in the protestant societies of the Early Modern Age, where every soldier was an expendable slave to be dressed up, paraded and shot, masculinity stood as a barrier to total domestication and the breaking of the captive soul, such that by 1800, legal action was being taken in the United States to limit the ability of a grateful owner to release his slaves from bondage. Even George Washington was foiled in his plan to release his black slaves by the disloyalty of his wicked widow.

The Hero

'What about Religion and Fighting?' A Man Question from Steevo Bristol

"Dude, what is up with all of these MMA fighters giving Jesus the credit for the win? Is this something new?"
-Steevo

Steevo, the first prize-fighters were all regarded as heroes and their contests were considered in a similar light later attributed to the suffering of Jesus on the cross. The very name for an ancient athletic contest we overlook, as we, as materialistic pleasure and safety seekers think in terms of things and access to things rewarded.

Athlete means "prize-seeker" in the language of the ancient Hellenic pankratists and boxers, which were the counterparts of our current combat athletes.

So, although such men did seek to win prizes [mostly just symbolic laurel wreathes] the event they engaged in was known as an *agon,* and their preparations for this *agonistics,* from which we have received the term *agony,* meaning suffering.

These men were seen as representing the spirit of their community and family as they contended with others, literally before the altars of a pantheon of gods that were considered cruel, not loving like the Jesus proclaimed by current Christian prize-fighters.

Although these contests were brutal and fighters did occasionally die, death was not the intent and since they were intrinsically sacrificial, if a fighter died it was considered a victory for him and the man who he fought against was fined.

Not all heroes were considered 'good' some being downright evil, such as a disqualified fighter who tore down the roof over a group of school children, killing them.

The important thing about a hero was that he literally challenged the gods[1], which, in ancient Hellenic thinking, places Jesus Christ as a hero, who defied the gods of his people's masters in Rome and likewise defied the priesthood of his own people. Most Christian doctrine places Jesus as a heroic figure, an actual sacrifice, so there is no contradiction in seeing him as an inspiration to athletes or even soldiers. Christianity was originally accepted as the Roman

---

[1] If you are an atheist or agnostic and are trying to wrap your head around this concept, think of challenging the gods in terms of challenging Fate, nature or some previously impassable barrier, such as a mountain, an ocean or outer space.

state religion under Constantine based largely on its effectiveness as a sacrificial religion, in motivating soldiers. When this Romanized form of Christianity was brought to 1500s Mexico, and its bloody-handed proponents defeated the Aztecs, who had the most sacrificially-inclined religion and society know to historians, conversion of the Aztec survivors to Catholicism became one of the greatest success stories in Christian history.

Just as the hero-cultists of first century Greece—who literally worshipped inspirational persons who had sacrificed themselves in defiance, such as Socrates the Philosopher, or risked life and social status battling a predatory rape cult, such as Euthymus the boxer—often favored the idea of an aspect of God [in this case his son] suffering in human form, the Aztec warriors, all willing to be sacrificed for the good of their nation, also identified with this agonized interpretation of the divine, a sentiment obvious in the heroic conduct and crowd-pleasing style of Mexican boxers to this day. The bravery of Mexican boxers is so common it may be regarded as a national characteristic in terms of that sport.

It is important to recall that in the ancient view a hero faces enemies within [traitors and his own self-doubts, as did Jesus as portrayed in the Gospels] and crucially enemies from without, usually rendered in mythic terms as monsters such as Humbaba or Grendel [and in the Gospels as the evil world, which passes sentence on and kills Jesus for his teachings.]

If looked at coldly, in secular, literary terms, the life and sacrifice of Jesus may be seen as a form of heroization and later deification of the condemned counter-culture leader, like Socrates. However, looked upon from the Christian perspective, by a masculine combatant, the idea of a non-combatant suffering and dying for a higher purpose, has had great motivating appeal to fighting men for at least the past 1700 years. Our social forms might change, but individually-combative men [as opposed to a mob or a unit of slave soldiers] have remained motivationally much the same across the ages.

In my view, there is nothing more evocative of the ancient heroic tradition across numerous warrior cultures, in the northern hemispheres of the new and ancient worlds, than the prize-fighters, exemplified by Catholic and protestant boxers and MMA fighters crediting their victory to God, often, specifically in the form of Jesus Christ.

Is it as simple as a belief in a higher power buoying the spirit of a fighter or is it more?

In this man's mind it is one and the same.

'Are You a Rightist or a Leftist?'

A Man Question from Jerome

Jerome, politically I am neither Right, Left or Centrist, but an outlier mind and alienated person. I do not have a place on the political continuum.

Culturally, since both ends of the political spectrum want to tell me what to do, I distrust them both.

However, the central position is compromising to such a degree as to amount to moral and spiritual erasure.

Since I engage socially–such as through writing–I am not outside the cultural continuum.

Culturally I see the Right and the Left in a race to the bottom of Negation.

On the Right, there has, for about 400 years [let's say beginning in 1618-48, with the Thirty Years War], been a concerted effort to negate all culture that falls outside of the Judeo-Christian model. The protestant reformation, for instance, was an attempt to purge indigenous European tradition from Christianity and was extended to the deconstruction and eradication of

Native American culture, culminating in the Carlisle School for Indian Children in the late 1800s. The Congregationalists of New England saw themselves as the new metaphysical Jews founding a "New Israel in these goings down of the sun," in reversal of the sins of Jews [in denying Jesus] and Christians [in embracing pagan concepts via Catholicism] and towards the end of eradicating heathens and the uncultivated natural ecology that sustained them, thus returning the world to its proper garden like state of domestication. Implicit in this process is an erosion of masculinity embedded in the domestication ethos, which some Christian thinkers address to varying degrees in such books as John Eldredge's *Wild at Heart*.

On the Left, for about the last 200 years [let's say the French Revolution, 1795-1815], there has been a concerted effort to negate Christianity and Masculinity, both of which bracket the deeper pagan traditions, one succeeding the other, preceding traditional European and Native American cultures. In many ways masculinity is the font of culture, as the rituals for making a man out of a suddenly dangerous youth are among the oldest customs traceable from early modern to stone-age societies.

The combined effect is cultural negation across the board. So, whether it's some bleeding heart Left-winger hiding out with an Amazonian tribe trying to help them preserve their way of life or some Right-wing Christian trying to preserve what decency has been left to him, or a Right-wing paleo-culturalist tying to resurrect ancient European heathenry, I identify with them all, because they are all doing something to preserve human culture in the face of the Thing that seeks to devour our individual and collective identities.

So, Jerome, I would have to say that, since two of the three types of people I identify with are to the Right of lethal compromise and one is to the Left of that same dark pit, I'm in ideological orbit, in poor communication with one human faction and in imperfect communication with the other, as they take turns plying the Devil's knives of negation upon each other's identities in service to Ultimate Nothingness.

Note

I would say that most of Americans are Center, fewer are Left and the least are Right.

Apolitical or Asshole?

'James, Are You Really Anti-American, Really?' – Jeremy Bentham

Two of my fighters and three of my coworkers have asked me this question since the Great Divisive Election of 2016—the American Schism if you will.

One of the things I like about our readership is the agreement to disagree, which makes me de facto part of the "Alternative-Right." This I do not like, because in my political heart—which I only give voice to in fiction—I view even white nationalists as whining liberals. I tolerate this Rightist designation for the very simple reason that people on the liberal, bleeding-heart Left are operating from a feminine axis and are incapable, fundamentally, of agreeing to disagree. I believe this is fundamental to the human condition and that we, meaning members of civilized societies of the West, are doomed to live along an increasingly feminine axis for two reasons:

1. In modern, civilized societies women outnumber men, and hence a democratic-republican model of government will naturally

result in a consensus based, safety-first, feminist society.

2. Civilization feminizes men on the chemical level. Look around you at the 20-year-old men of today, pear-shaped behemoths to narrow-shouldered twerps.

I see it as a done deal until something occurs to plunge us back into barbarism, which is the natural cycle of our kind—thus far—a cycle that the feminist construct seeks to break.

I see my place as a chronicler of this process and a historian of the overall cycle, in that I am writing for my grandsons.

I regard myself as dead, or rather undead, a husk. I have no more ambition to fight, fuck, make money, coach, organize, network or make money or make money or make money...

I regard myself as someone hanging round for the good of my kin, fighters and friends, who I always assist when they ask.

I do not think I have—as someone who has quit living, as our society defines it—a moral right to participate in politics. I further think that such participation would muddy my judgment and make me a less accurate documentarian of our critical decline.

I know it seems bizarre that I seem to trumpet Trump, who stands for making America great again, when I myself decry America as evil.

I like Trump—despite having always disliked him and continuing to dislike him—out of respect for challenging the vast beast that shall probably devour him—which will eat even the memory of him and cough it up as a lie. I also value Trump as possibly the most important historical figure in American history since Abraham Lincoln.

Yes, I believe in my heart and in my mind, that America is and has always been evil, in that it is a vehicle for proxy aggression, a massive emotionally bound social construct that permits disgusting little faggots and shrill whores to tell real men how to live—The State ultimately permits the dysgenic waste of humanity to not only apply monstrous force to those few surviving human souls, but also contrive their diminishment. I only prefer America to all other evil nations—and all nations are fundamentally evil beyond redemption—because I have loved ones in the land claimed by that evil beast.

No, I am not a Libertarian who believes the State is evil because it is an instrument of aggression, I'm a simple human being who knows that the State is evil because it puts power in the hands of spiritually powerless people, making worm-like creatures, such as Tolkien's ring wraiths, of all, utterly corrupted by contact with power beyond their ken—only our voter-wraiths are worse than Tolkien's Nazgul, for they all believe themselves engaged in a greater good. At least Sauron's boys knew they were the bad guys.

Yes, I am superstitious, to a far greater degree than I will normally admit.

Yes, I am, by common definition, an asshole, and I like our current president solely on the grounds that he is nearly the perfect asshole.

And yes, I am apolitical—though I have had to check my conscience and resist voting for the lesser of two evils, otherwise I would not be able to continue writing commentary on current events without feeling like a hypocrite, which to a writer is far worse than being one.

In the meantime, I mean no disrespect to our many conservative and right-wing readers when I write such heartfelt sympathies as, "I wish the Wicked Witch of the Left would have won the election so that I could see Russian and U.S. aviators downing each other over Syria," or "If I had a time machine I'd shoot George Washington in the head while the signatories of your sacred documents burned to death in the room he locked them into to hammer out the details of my domestication."

Jeremy, thank you so much for all your work, and for representing the American patriots who come to this site despite the ungrateful asshole whose slave name is blazed across the header.

To hell with peace, give War a try—but do it civilly, please, for I much prefer a ringside seat.

Thank you all—even the guy that's going to take his 'like' down off of the Facebook page.

Jeremy Bentham comments:

Conservatives adapt to the world they live in. Leftists want to change the world to suit themselves.

- John J. Ray (M.A.; Ph.D.) Brisbane, Australia, Dissecting Leftism BlogSpot.

There are no morals in politics; there is only expedience. A scoundrel may be of use to us just because he is a scoundrel.

- Vladimir Ilyich Lenin

Survival cancels programing.

- Ted Cassidy as Ruk the Android, "What Little Girls Are Made Of", Star Trek.

James, you've just identified a major difference between the Right and the Left. Contrary to the Left promoted stereotype, we Right-wingers are actually more capable of being able to accept and appreciate people and things for what they are, rather than what we might wish they were. Unlike Leftists, we Right-wingers don't feel compelled to change the whole world to suit us. Thus we Alt-Right-wingers tend to appreciate you for the contrary, Darwinist cave-man you are. We would simply know enough not to put you out of your element, and say, place you in charge of the Louvre, where you would chop up the Mona Lisa for firewood. Now the Left on the other hand would insist that a fringe person like you be put in charge of something important like the Louvre. We Right-wing Conservatives would insist that this was a really bad idea, because you would chop up the Mona Lisa and goodness knows what other priceless art treasures. Nevertheless the Left would refuse to listen to us and accuse us of being mean-spirited just for stating the facts of the matter. "Well even if James said he would chop up the Mona Lisa, I'm sure he didn't really mean it, once he's in the room with her he'll see how beautiful she is." "Besides", the Left would say, "he needs a better life and a better job than he has now, he can't possibly be happy getting hit in the head every day like he does at his boxing gym." So the Left would put you in charge of the Louvre where you'd promptly chop up and burn the Mona Lisa and nobody would be happy with the outcome. But naturally the Left would try to blame the mess on the Right. "What did you do to him you evil Right-wingers? Somebody must have done something to James as a child that he would act like this today." "Well maybe so", the Right would retort, "but we didn't do it to him and we weren't the dumb-asses who put an unmanageable misfit like him in charge of the Louvre either! He was doing fine as a boxing and stick-fighting coach and writing his fringe literature. You should have left him there." So then the Left would make you a yoga instructor, or something else where they'd imagine you couldn't do too much damage. They wouldn't let you go back to boxing and stick–fighting, that's for sure, but you'd set up an underground fight club in the yoga studio anyway.

The author responds: I meant it, JB, I'd chop her up, mustache and all!

Thank you for the analysis and defaulting to the better angels of my nature.

The Hero King

What Kind of Societal Figurehead Fits a Tribal, Masculine and Transcendent Worldview?

Written with the thoughts on a just society, as expressed by Joseph Bellofatto over the course of our friendship.

The modern president or prime minister is a subdued shadow of the classical king, just as the dictator is a feminized caricature of the king, expressive or collectively distorted to the point of celebrity.

The classical king, himself, is nothing more than a pale imitation of the hero king, seduced by material concerns, managed by moneyed puppets as far back as the Magna Carta of 1215. Hence, even the king of the High Middle Ages is a debased commodity, and a manipulated manipulator, an evolved inheritor of Agamemnon, not of Achilles

A hero king, like the hero he was before assuming kingship—David comes to mind—must, by definition be a hero first, a man who went against the established order. In an infinitely corrupt and degraded way, a modern businessman who went against the political order would satisfy this requirement. In most cases, the hero turned king is ruined by his transformation, but the ruin is his, as a sacrificial figure, rather than the ruin of the nation that befalls the followers of a dictator or a managerial head of state.

For a view of the heroic conflict of interest with the duties of kingship, one should read *The Rage of Achilles* from the *Iliad* and the Prologue of *Beowulf*. As both the conflict between hero and king take their toll on the nation and army respectively, as the King is essentially illegitimate in masculine, meaning primal, terms, with his stature based upon the accumulated wealth passed down by hero kings and passed upward by slave subjects, resting upon the actual heroism—actionist sacrifice—of politically disenfranchised henchmen. This latter element reflects the essential instability of any hereditary kingship and the illegitimate proxy nature of any politically selected head-of-state.

Recently, while discussing politics and my apolitical lack of alignment with a war-fighter, he asked me why I could neglect an attempt to influence the selection of the regime leadership that my sons must live under.

I responded that my position was so far to the right that alignment with the New American Political Right made no more sense to me than the alignment of the "Alt-Right" with third wave feminist political candidates would make to writers at such sites as

Counter-Currents and VDare, and that the very idea of a president serving as the hood ornament of an ostensible oligarchy, which is in fact the backroom-bought mask of an actual plutocratic state, was a political form so intrinsically corrupt and false-faced that no good could come of it.

He then asked what kind of government I would support.

I put forth the idea of the Hero King:

- The man must have fought;
- The man must have killed;
- The man must give away all his worldly possessions;
- The man must then engage in some physical contest to be named king;
- The man must serve uncompensated, advised by older, not younger, men, who have likewise sworn an oath of poverty;
- The man must participate in any military action he initiates;
- The man must retire into poverty and exile when physical or mental decline render him ineffective.

That is it, rather than a hero becoming degraded by kingship and devolving into the pawn that pushes lesser pawns around the board of death merchant exchange, he should remain the bane of such manipulators, rather than surrender to their embrace as any modern head-of-state must.

James, I can just hear the objections: "A man who has killed?!" But our presidents do kill, by giving orders from their desks. Wouldn't it be better if that man had the perspective that comes from committing the act with his own hands? James, your requirements for a fit ruler are consistent with the idea that a just society can only be a small society. Our massive global order must suppress the individual humanity of its subjects or it will crumble.

-Lynn

Lynn, tribal societies can confederate up, maintain a decent society on the local level and elect a Commander in Chief who only has war powers, such as the Irish did to break the Vikings at Clontarf under King Brian Boru in 1014, a battle in which a king did everything a king should do, including die in the defense of his nation.

https://en.wikipedia.org/wiki/Battle_of_Clontarf

The king is by definition a confederated tribal leader. Until gunpowder technology rendered multiethnic armies [with each tribe bringing a troop type specialty to build a combined arms team] obsolete, permitting military formations to be "mono-cropped" [something that had been very hard for the Romans to achieve in the era of muscle-powered weapons], kings were best served, in terms of military needs, by having unique and diverse contingents under their rule. With the industrialization of warfare, army building could be conducted as the management of interchangeable units, much like a modern economy.

The moral component is key, that the king has fought and killed. This is why proxy wars are so nasty and why queens wage war far more often than kings, which is ultimately tied to the higher level of aggression by females in managerial positions and behind the wheels of vehicles, as human females are maladapted to the possession of lethal force.

'A Bunch of Nazis?'

A Cautionary Tale of Tested Association

Note to reader: This piece was posted publicly on July 2, 2017, weeks before the events in Charlottesville, Virginia on August 12, 2017, where a "Unite the Right Rally," including at least some participants claiming to be white nationalists and carrying Nazi flags, clashed with Antifa counterdemonstrators, resulting in the death of one counterdemonstrator. Reports indicate that Antifa had tacit support from local law enforcement and came ready for battle. See also the events in Berkeley, California in April of 2017.

A couple weeks ago a reader contacted me concerning an associate of his who will be coming through the Baltimore Area later this summer. He wanted to know if I would be able to arrange security and a low-risk venue for this man, who simply wished to give a slide show presentation of black-on-white violence in his hometown. I was assured that he was not a white nationalist, just a concerned member of a beleaguered community.

I indicated that I would know within two weeks if this could be arranged.

Since the date given would be a weekend, bar accommodations could not be arranged.

Mescaline Franklin told me he would come into town for this event and pay the cover fee for the venue, so long as it was in the hundreds and not the thousands.

The meeting we wished to facilitate would be a brief evening event. So, with expenses covered, I went about this in the old fashioned way.

I would be seeking space in a gym or dojo, six of which I have ties to.

The three mixed-race gyms are out, not because the black fighters would mind—they are in the gym to escape a similar situation—but because the small group of assembled people might have to conduct their meeting in the presence of a black man punching a bag. Seriously, such gyms are mostly run by fighter-coaches, who will come in during the off hours for their solo work, as business hours occupy them with coaching.

That left me with three locations, three men I know. None of these three men do business on the phone, it's a handshake or nothing, even with friends. None of them use email.

One of these men dislikes me, as three of his fighters left him to train with me.

This man grumbled something barely audible about non-fighters defiling his sacred combat space. Honesty, I lost this one on my personality and history with this guy, because he could have used some extra money and was recently forced to move his dojo to a more expensive site because of black-on-white violence.

One man was not able to commit to the date because of a previous scheduled commitment—a belt test, I think, although he didn't bother explaining.

The third man, deeply in need of rent money for his under-attended school, looked at me in amazement tinged with fear, "What, you wanna bring a bunch of Nazis into my place?"

I groaned, having hit the proverbial wall.

The lessons here for me, are three:

1. Even though most Alt-Right supporters are hard-working men who may expect to be busy during the week, since Antifa brats play hardest on the weekend, and bars [which are often closed on Monday or Tuesday and could be rented in advance] do booming business on weekends, a weekday evening should be considered rather than a weekend, early in the week or midweek, preferred.

2. That such events need to be planned 8-12 weeks in advance, not 4-6 weeks.

3. Gyms and Dojos are now also submerged in the PC matrix, even on the rough fringe. Even men who are being squeezed out of business and their masculine arts abandoned as physical autonomy is removed from the social value set by this

feminization of considered community into shrill pecking order, have already internalized the fear that is the currency of the masculine invalidation system we live under.

Although I was unable to assist with securing a venue, if this man still comes to Baltimore, I have offered to assist with his personal security, confident that he is committed to a low-profile exposition of his views.

Post Charlottesville

Anarcho-Tyranny Endgame

I watched the Kovalev-Taylor fight six months ago and saw Kovalev beat this guy from post to post. Then, last month, I saw the HBO edited version of the highlights, which took 36 minutes of action, what I knew was a one-sided beating of Taylor, and presented as five minutes of Taylor hammering Kovalev!

So, as Alt-Right protesters get better and better at defending themselves they will be depicted on the news as becoming more and more effective aggressors, mad dog Nazis terrorizing the Good People of the Nation.

News from Charlottesville confirms that the rally was a set-up, with cops actually pushing Alt-Right protestors into their attackers once the permit was revoked–which was another bit of skullduggery. However, as I'm writing this I am viewing network news, which convincingly depicts, for the brainwashed masses, who live on the video soundbite and are immune to facts, an army of White Nationalists and White Supremacists–artfully stamping one term with the older label–slaughtering innocents. No sooner than the news was over and a comedian was crying about the slaughter of the innocents, a Trump impersonator was dancing on a talent show and the MC was reminding audience members to vote.

But just as the masses cannot see fact, the Alt-Right can't see consequences.

The scared kid in the car who was being attacked by a bat wielding mob and ran over some of his attackers, killing one, is likely to be acquitted due to the evidence.

In the meantime, White Nationalists will continue to provide footage of the White Supremacists army, as unpaid stuntmen for their enemies.

The end game is simple, when that kid gets acquitted, it will mean riots in every majority black American city. This time, since white men have been identified as the aggressors, it will not just be cops standing by while a city like Baltimore is raped and scorched, but cops lending a hand to the criminals as they both converge on their shared prey.

Post Script

This morning, after finishing this piece, I walked out into my sister's front yard in deep suburban Maryland in Harford County and found the local newspaper, the Aegis, with the front page story being a 20-person support rally for the victims of the Nazi Stormtroopers who crushed freedom and struck a blow for "oppression." There was a token black couple with a BLM poster. The rest were the brainwashed palefaces who hate themselves for being born in evil skin and feel the need to lash out at those who embrace their evil Caucasian nature.

This is the endgame of the years of leftist attacks on peaceful rightist speakers, to garner footage of aggressive white men out of uniform, to usher in the idea that unapologetic white men are the enemy of all, even of themselves.

Action versus Reaction

What Any Boxer Could Have Told the Alt-Right

Action typically beats reaction.

There are exceptions.

If you are bigger than the actor, then your reaction—provided you survived the action—may overwhelm him.

If you are much more skilled and experienced in the arena you do combat in, then you have predicted the actor's action and set him up for failure and might do a cut-off punch, a stop hit, an interception. One of the smarter martial artists of the 1960s, Bruce Lee, termed his art, Jeet Kune Do, which means way of the intercepting fist, or being an order of magnitude better prepared.

The normal advantage in any contest is to be had when the more powerful party—think Mike Tyson in his prime—leads and the opponent is left reacting to his actions, thus, even when he is successful one action at a time, in the overall conduct of the contest he is following, not leading, actually subject to the course of events as if he were in a storm.

The disaster scenario is when the more powerful and more experienced party [the mainstream Liberal establishment] commits an action to draw a reaction from a tiny outgunned foe, so that the underdog will make himself available to be smashed. When such an underdog, new to the method of conflict, then charges in, the result is always a crushing defeat. The Fetterman Massacre, conducted by Crazy Horse, comes to mind.

So, in a political contest between liberals who hold most government posts at all levels of the judicial and legislative structures, and dominate executive positions in the cities where such riots resulting from rank-and-file disturbances might occur, and traditionalists, who hold no offices and are even a tiny minority in the sphere of ideas, any reaction by the traditionalists to the actions of liberals is like the tiny reaction to the movement of the massive beast of state to the left, eliciting a reaction that is like a fly bite, which can be expected to bring the tail of that beast whipping around to squash the irritating insect on its rump.

Just a boxing thought for those who might want to think outside the box.

Bitch Parade

Post-postscript to Masculine Axis: Subverting the Masculine Triumph by Feminizing Ancient Forms of Upright Assembly

Forms of seated assembly, such as councils are not under discussion here, but rather those forms of public assembly traditionally engaged in by military age men.

The triumphal or solemn procession, from dances reenacting the slaying of a beast by the returning hunter, to Roman triumphs and the funerary procession of slain heroes and symbolic conduction of the dead, the history of humans conducting group displays in an organized fashion to illustrate, celebrate or show reverence for action is rich.

Our parade traditions come down to us from the ancient hunters through these postwar and funerary sources and have coalesced in three degraded forms:

1. The holiday parade, to celebrate civic spirit and culture.

2. The military review, used by martially oriented governments to awe and impress subjects and enemies alike.

3. Ideological marches, from breast cancer awareness to political protests.

All three of these modern forms are derived from the Roman triumph, with funerary processions remaining in form, if not substance, essentially the same. The three forms above represent:

1. A neutered triumph in the form of the holiday parade, a celebration of **being** rather than **doing**.

2. A corrupted form of the triumph in the form of a threat of victory rather than a confirmation of victory, boasting rather than doing.

3. Protest, strike and support marches and vigils, which are an entirely feminine interpretation of the triumph, with the protestors serving a sacrificial function, placing themselves there to be victimized by those unjustly in power and garner sympathy for their cause.

A discussion of the last is in order, as it has been transmogrified into a trivial battlefield over which traditionally feminized protestors have attempted and failed to draw police action and build sympathy for the political left. However, the attempt by emasculated males of the various Alt-Right and White Nationalist alliances to vent their fury over the destruction of their culture and society has now caused an interesting turn of events. The Left, who had thus far failed to draw police attacks to build solidarity through the media with the brainwashed herd of Americans, managed to provoke counter-attacks from the Right, which drew in police action. For once, sympathy after such a clash is with the Leftist agitators and the police, with the Right–who had been attempting to use a debased celebration platform, coopted for a feminist-slave agenda, as a base for masculine expression–managing to place themselves as enemies of the Left and police [who have heretofore served and have been seen as an iconic aspect of the American Right], solidifying and unifying mainstream support for a Leftist police state.

Whoever facilitated this at the highest levels, which means people unseen and unknown to the Alt-Right organizers, pulled a classic piece of political dupemanship, with the Right rank and file, expecting to stand together with the police against the Left being caught between a rock and sick place.

The Left turn of the police in this manner, while highly predictable, represents the greatest change in American public life since 1865.

After past clashes I have fielded questions on the mechanics of such encounters, noting that victory for the Right in such a staged fight was the worst possible outcome. I expect that men on the Right, wanting to do even better in future clashes with the Left will send me links of such footage. I will decline to comment other than to use such clashes as studies for examining ancient combat. As for advice on how to "win" against a pack of vicious freaks, with the prize of being labelled a Nazi and being crushed by police–and if that doesn't work National Guard, and if that doesn't work DOJ contractors–I will offer no combat advice.

Understand that the American Right lost at Charlottesville. The Left, the voting public, Law Enforcement and Government are all now firmly aligned.

If you believe in liberty, if you believe in family, if you believe in decency, if you believe that manhood is important, if you believe that being proud of having great ancestors is worth fighting for, then fighting again now will bring you the wages of Carthage, the salting of your earth and the erasure of your people.

The only chance for liberty and identity is in the future, after some societal collapse. For now, the most that can be done is to record and keep a real history, to speak against the lies our children will be weaned on, to preserve a body of masculine knowledge that may serve as the seed of a new society rising from the ashes of this mass of corruption known as modernity.

The American Right lost any chance of having a legitimate political voice in Pre-Collapse America, on Saturday, August 12 2017.

The Scale of Warfare

Q&A with James LaFond (JL) & Lynn Lockhart (LL)

Masculine Revival in the Face of the Machine State: From the Peace of Westphalia to the Marseilles Soccer Hooligan Clash and the Baltimore Riots

LL: James, you recently reviewed a video, *Russia's Hooligan Army,* in your piece, *No Small Beer*. The video is an hour long and well worth watching, but the gist of it is that there is a growing movement of Soccer Hooliganism in Russia. Young men are training and fighting one another in groups, and in 2016, around 200 of these Hooligans went to Marseilles during the World Cup and attacked their English counterparts. English Hooliganism has seen better days and they were unaware and unprepared for the battle. The video was put out by the BBC and has the predictable biases.

James, you have observed that the Peace of Westphalia marked the beginning of "national machine warfare." Relatedly, Nassim Taleb has proposed, also citing the Peace of Westphalia, in *Antifragile* that the existence of nation-states, as opposed to city-states, feudal and tribal groups, led to the pattern of war of the twentieth century, with large scale conflict, and has left the world with far greater danger of catastrophic war than ever in history. This contrary to the popular view (from Steven Pinker) that violence, including warfare, is on the decline worldwide. Taleb's point is that having numerous local skirmishes is much safer than having large powers in constant tension, and we won't know how bad it could get until it does.

JL: Lynn, first, violence within society continues to increase, counter to law enforcement data. Society is now more violent per foot space than it ever was. However, since our intellectuals deal in violence per 100,000 residents, an intrinsically dehumanized scale, we, like the wildebeest, are seen as rarely preyed upon. Medieval studies of violence show a high per-capita rate of violence. However, per-capita notions are artificial. What is important is violence per square foot. How dangerous is the place where you live if you removed everybody but yourself and the predators? That is the psychologically impactful view, what produces alcoholism, drug addiction, suicide, ennui, decadence.

Furthermore, if we go along with the misleading and fundamentally flawed FBI notion of macro-data qualified violence we see the following when compared with my first hand survey:

- In 1996, only 25% of violence came to the attention of law enforcement.
- In 2016, only 5% of violence came to the attention of law enforcement.

During this 20 year period law enforcement has made a multi-layered commitment to reclassifying violence down, with home invasions becoming destruction of property, muggings becoming theft, etc.

Beyond this is the fact that most aggression does not result in legally definable aggression. Me following you to your car and then walking on by because your husband happens to be sitting in the car, when if he hadn't been I would have attacked you, is not definable by law enforcement.

Also, where murders may remain stagnant, with handgun killings staying steady nationwide and stabbing perhaps doubling, blunt force attacks, as the admittance of clubbing and beating victims do not trigger law enforcement responses as do gunshot, stabbing and rape admittances, have greatly increased, with cagey criminals averse to prison time switching to blunt force away from firearms and edged weapons.

Taking the above factors, from Baltimore City, into account, how can anyone look at a marginal decrease in overall killing rates across the nation, or a reduction of robbery rates [which are heavily massaged by reporting methods] and see a less violent world, where it is at least three times as violent?

A better way to rate aggression would be to track the sale and installation of plexi-glass counter shields at retail outlets and aggregate them, meaning the bulletproof counter installed on North and Maryland 40 years ago is still in use, and all of those built since, at an accelerating rate, actually amount to a manifold doubling of hostile points of aggression and predation across the real physical landscape rather than in the contrived theoretic landscape of the FBI macro stats.

As for the Peace of Westphalia, which traditionally dates the rise of the nation state, projecting force with conscription-based armies over kingdoms and republics employing feudal obligations and mercenary employment for force projection, here are my immediate thoughts.

The defeat of the Spanish tercios [combined arms regiments loyal to the king of Spain] that led to the Peace of Westphalia, killed whatever connection to heroism that warfare, that is whatever the brutal Thirty Years' War had not already erased. In a very real sense, that war, from 1618 to 1648 was when God was killed on the battlefield along with the divine right of kingship. Kings would now increasingly become a class of managerial despot compromised by their advisors. That war also saw the first weapons of mass destruction, the Hell-Burner of Antwerp. The Spanish were as evil as the rest of the players. But their soldiery still held to notions of heroism that would soon only find expression in dueling and prize fighting, which emerged at this very time as a plague on the officer class. We see honorable violence being pushed downward into society as the first modern slave armies [they emptied the prisons and whore houses to fill the ranks] sterilized war of meaning as it became a collective expedient.

LL: James, do you think the Russian Soccer Hooligans represent a return to tribal warfare? You point out in the comments to that article that these firms fight one another for practice. By fighting firm vs. firm, they signal the safety of their towns, and by joining up to fight the English, they can also signal national strength.

JL: The fact is that these hooligans are engaging in warrior pursuits with meaning as only a few hundred men of any nation can engage in meaningful warrior activity in the machine-minded armed services. Once you get below the special operations types you just have a welfare state-prison-school-system in uniform.

LL: I have mixed feelings about what they did in Marseilles, but I wonder if there aren't a few English and French who would think twice now about going to war with Russia?

JL: Such notions as national will for war are really obsolete. War is now a machined wraith of its former self, a form of macro-policing by globalists and doomed resistance by nationalists, and has been such since 1948. This Marseilles clash was about the Russians using the occasion to assert their masculine humanity over the decadent Brits, in essence saying, "We will remain Russians and men, as you are thrown on the scrap heap of humanity by the soulless system that your grandfathers fought to erect, which has now begun eating its own, reducing you to neither men or Englishmen, but a shadow without a ghost—you revolted against Modernity and sank into sloth and we carry on."

The Russians are letting the British and the dying West know that they have all become like Tolkien's ring wraiths—terminally, amorally domesticated ciphers.

LL: Looking back over this I have left out what I really wanted to talk about which is your idea about outsourcing violence.

We can see that an individual man has the right to risk his own body in the violent endeavors of his choosing. You have made your life's work out of sharing your violent experiences, and we learned about some of the physical consequences in your book *Winter of a Fighting Life*.

By joining firms, these young Russian men compromise themselves to a group, albeit a small and highly accountable one. The leaders of the group are fighting alongside the recruits and we saw that the fighting and the leading are inextricably linked when Vasily indicated that he had retired from fighting and firm leadership, without distinguishing between the two. Moving up the scale any further removes the warrior role from the leaders who are responsible for disposing of their lives.

JL: Lynn, you have just described a real—if circumscribed within the confines of modernity—a real, actualized return to the hero bands of primal antiquity. Vasily and his men are Gilgamesh and Enkidu, Odysseus and his Crew, Jason and his Argonauts, Achilles and his Myrmidons and Beowulf and his dozen heroes. As strange as it seems Russian soccer Hooliganism is a protest against a society based on outsourced aggression and an expressed yearning for a return to a primal lifestyle.

LL: Thank you James.

Anarcho-Tyranny Patrolling

A Man Question from Mescaline Franklin

"Let's say you've got five or six families living on a block and the men want to keep it safe, what then would you suggest as procedures? I know you're inclined to say don't organize openly, but you're a pioneer when it comes to surviving in the shitty environments that the Chosen are determined to make our cities into."

-Mescaline Franklin

One, you never patrol as a full group because that 1) marks you out as vigilantes and invites the hammer, 2) means you aren't covering most the time slots, 3) puts the families in danger of being totally unprotected if all five guys get rounded up by the pigs.

You need intelligence the most: who is threatening who and where are they coming from?

If they're around the corner, that's an entirely different thing than dealing with raiders, which is most of what I deal with.

One big drawback in terms of being targeted by the pigs is that gangs and do-it-yourself tribes tend to be based on masculine and racial identity and include no outliers, which retards intelligence and makes you easy to spot. Destroying the family is the smartest thing the State ever did. What you need is men of different ages, from older teens to seniors working intelligence gathering, baiting soft comers—the rookies and newbies and prospects that get sent out on raids to prove themselves—and identify and ward off the hard comers.

If you are Asians, or Latinos or Jews, or some other group who is allowed to mass and share identity, unlike gentile whites—I know it's not fair but it is what it is—then you can actually lobby politicians, ask for police advice, all kinds of stuff. But if you are white you are not permitted to act as a group. Governments like to remain alive and growing and the people who took down just about every government that ever got got, looked like you and me.

After intelligence: identifying threats by frequency, severity and target, then you need to patrol in a low key fashion, old man walking with his cane during the morning, two young adults together, but physically separate[1] during clutch raiding times and the guys with messed up schedules filling in the gaps. Just being a neighborhood where there is always an able bodied and attentive man visible and moving about, takes your residential area off of criminal hit lists and means you mainly have to make nice with the pigs, who shouldn't be a problem unless you swarm some crook.

I know that this whole neo-masculinity, tribalism thing that we are a part of, one way or the other, says that you pack up and act like ancient douchebag warriors. But that is just stupid.

You are fighting an insurgency as an insurgency with no conventional backup. You have two enemies that tend not to complement each other, so your priority needs to be avoiding setting it up so you get smashed between.

Let's say five of you beat the piss out of a sainted Dindu who was only trying to ask the old lady for the time and was only smacking her so she would raise her voice—brutha's got a right to the time you know—then his people come after your people while you are all in jail. And who pays for defending five guys?

---

[1] Two guys together are magnets for mob strength packs and gun-armed trios and foursomes. You are better off being in visual contact, but not in the arc that can be covered by one handgun.

What you want is one guy doing the work and the rest serving as witnesses or legal fee donators.

Think like a criminal, act like a concerned citizen and don't forget who sent the Dindus–the same people who will send the police if you maim or kill or act out on video. Your instinct might be to gather in a group–and since this is a bitch nation that bitch instinct makes sense. But you never pack up in a mass right in front of a heavy piece of ordinance, which is what that smart phone in the hand of the mugger's friend is, the Eye of Government-as-God.

Koanic comments:

The problem of how to build cohesion out of atomized men remains. It's a Millennial problem which you may not appreciate, but for us it's quite real.

What you describe requires cohesion. It would be good to know how to build that.

The author responds:

I deal with a lot of millennial emasculation as a boxing and weapons coach.

As a loner type, I am not qualified to offer cohesion advice for the normal man, only for those of my type—who have their own need to augment and serve cohesive groups. I am just trying to make the human bricks stronger. Someone else will have to build the wall.

For unit building you should look to ball sports like rugby and to group fighting formats like what those Russian soccer hooligans do I the fields in Russia.

Jeremy Bentham comments:

I am sending you out like sheep among wolves. Therefore be as shrewd as snakes and as innocent as doves. Be on your guard.

Matthew 10:16-17 (NIV)

"Think like a criminal, act like a concerned citizen and don't forget who sent the Dindus—the same people who will send the police if you maim or kill or act out on video."

That is sage advice James. Ignore it your peril people! Yeah if the dindus manage to video tape you shouting the n-word in a confrontation with a dindu mob it's going to make it look like you started the fight when it is presented as evidence against you in court. Remember everybody out there has a smart phone/video camera nowadays.

The author responds:

Jeremy, military men like you, Baruch and others I am sure, understand how to build group cohesion. I'm a one on one coach just a guy shaping the man. I'd like it if you military men came up with some ideas on building small group cohesion.

Mitch the Coward

Squiggly Pork Update

Months ago I finally asked a customer who was, according to my instincts, a cop, if he was.

He almost had a heart attack.

I eventually comforted him into believing I wasn't a former victim of his police brutality or corruption, and we had a nice conversation, which I split into two articles posted at the time.

That was deep in the winter.

Mitch used to say "hi" to me every night and did so for five years.

Now, not only doesn't he say hello anymore, if he sees me in the aisle, he turns back around and does not make his purchase—the man is terrified of me, and he does not know I am a writer.

Three nights ago he actually shivered and spun on his heels, cutting his shopping trip short and slithering out the door.

Big Ron did give me an answer of sorts, reminding me that the Southwestern Precinct, where Mitch worked, was the most corrupt precinct in Baltimore for generations, and it has been generations.

Shoey told me about quitting selling heroin because after he picked up a kilo from the distributor, he found himself in a kitchen full of uniformed cops, snorting coke. This was in the Southwestern District.

Mitch failed one of those simple character tests, the ability to be a man.

Such simple, low pressure tests are the keys used by men to plot a map of the potential allies, foes and bystanders without doing anything other than extending a friendly word and a welcoming hand.

Mitch is off my map.

How Can We Protect Our Borders?

A Tribalist Wants To Know How a Free People Can Protect its Land

James, you seem to be a practical, anti-government thinker. I have discussions with tribal affiliates and anarchocapitalists about borders and it's like talking to libertarians about roads. Do you have any thoughts?

-Gene

First, Gene, think like a Marine or special ops soldier, not an Army administrator. Every military unit has a border that moves with it, like a cell wall moves with the innards of the cell. The border is the skin of the body politic and skin is not rigid, but porous.

In Korea the Marines on the right flank were overrun, just like the army on the left, by similar, overwhelming numbers of Chi-coms. The army melted because they fought and thought in terms of lines. The Marines just advanced in a new direction, fighting in their perimeter and retreated in good order, leaving no dead or wounded behind as the army had.

Throughout history nations have done a terrible job of protecting their borders due to their centralized nature, where tribal entities have survived enemy contact far longer. I interviewed three Marines and two army survivors of this same offensive and even though the Army's field favored their own American equipment and the Marine's mountainous battlefield favored Chinese infantry, the Marines had a unifying experience as the Army bugged out and collapsed.

Where Mexico fell to the predatory U.S. in months, the Apaches held out for 40 years against a better version of the same force.

Think of how many tribes crossed Roman borders, how many millions now stream across modern borders. The Amazonian tribes are doing a better job defending their borders than the U.S. ever has and most of our borders [the Atlantic and Pacific coasts] are impassable buy most types of armed forces.

States violate borders, it is intrinsic to their design. They have rarely been good at maintaining them, with such exceptions as Japan, Taiwan, and Switzerland being perimeter-oriented entities. If you organize a tribe, your only terminal fear will be a state-level force. The state was created as a way of amalgamating conquered tribes for the purpose of conquering more tribes, with the secondary purpose being wealth redistribution on a pyramidal model, and the tertiary purpose of the state coming into being with the advent of gunpowder slave armies, that being cultural negation.

For an ethno-nationalist, I suggest looking at medieval and ancient states that resisted empires and the compulsion to become an empire—for the imperial path leads to undefendable borders and disaster—the Germans, Picts and the Parthians for instance

A feudal model, which maximizes local resistance, but minimizes external force projection, worked better against Islamic pirates, for instance, than did empires, who were only suited for offense. The Roman eradication of piracy was internal, not external, and is not a good model. Instead look to the greater success the Japanese [with outdated technology] had over the British [with state-of-the-art technology] who had a terrible record against pirate raids for some 200 years even as they raided the ports of the larger Spanish polity with ease. Indeed, Ireland, with a more authentically tribal feudal structure than England, handled the Viking invaders much better—crushing them at Clontarf in 1013—preserving more territory and driving the Norse into the sea even as the English suffered proportionally more against the Danes, with the southern portion of Britain falling to successive waves of Saxons and Normans, in between suffering the indignities of the Danelaw.

Gene, tribal enclaves, such as Switzerland's cantons, and the clan-held valleys of Typee [which repulsed French invaders at a great technological disadvantage], are more sustainable than amalgamated nations. Look to Israel, which has much better control of its borders, even though it is surrounded by enemies, where the U.S. has little control over its own, more geographically remote [from invaders] borders.

Of course, there is also the fact that states have a nasty habit of exchanging native rights for immigrant rights, which accelerates border defense problems in order to feed the centralized parasitarchy.

Good luck with the tribe, Gene. You only have one enemy in this endeavor, the ultimate enemy, that which owns you, your children, your land and your acceptable measure of identity. Remember, simply being a white man is a crime in America, so you might, at least on the surface, identify your tribe in some other way, that is, until that which owns us dies from its intrinsic rot.

Now that you know who you are, know who they are.

Temperance

Missing the Point of Chemical Enslavement

Two friends of mine recently had a discussion about prohibition, one pointing out how stupid it was, the other coming to the defense of the Church ladies and other busybodies of America, and pointing out how rampant alcoholism was in industrial America.

The temperance advocate, who is also a drug war advocate, has missed one crucial point.

Why was alcoholism rampant in the first slave societies of Sumer and Egypt?

Why did Amerindians demonstrate such low tolerance for alcohol once introduced to it?

Why do almost all working class men in American cities self-medicate?

Why do most middle-aged American women, receive prescriptions for anti-depressants or anti-anxiety medications?

Because living in servitude, whether to the Priest-King or Pharaoh or to Modernity's intricately woven debt schemes, is a soul-crushing existence.

Miss Jenny's Eyes

A Guerilla Patriarchy Note

Miss Jenny gets off work at Overlea High School in Baltimore County and is forever stranded by the 9:40 bus, as her stop is dark and the drivers do not care to stop in unlighted areas, even as crime averse passengers avoid well-lighted hubs patrolled by thugs.

By 10:40, our driver spots her most of the time, as a male coworker holds a flashlight to mark her position. Since 2014 this Baltimore County school has become the hub of suburban ghettoization as students fan out and attack the Rosedale residents on the street and in their homes and police pretend these are burglaries and thefts. This school is also a major heroin distribution center.

Miss Jenny could barely contain herself after thanking the bus driver and began to regale us with tales of high school perversion that do not fit the fanciful matriarchy model of Black America:

"The pretty little girls are acting white, generally, maybe dating a man or what have you. But the big girls come to school half naked, everything hanging out. One was expelled today, breasts out of her bikini top. They got no more shape than a woman my age, but they let it *all* hang out.

"Every night I have to scrub the girls room wall of their gang signs and graffiti about big girls need lovin' too.

"These girls aspire to nothing more than popping out the babies of thugs, drug dealers and gang bangers. You can believe this ya'll, and best gather 'round 'cause I ain't sayin' it twice!

"It was during school hours. My day starts cleaning up after the first lunch period. I was walking down to the janitorial closet, on the basement level, past the back of the bottom stairwell, where it is deep and dark. I hear something and turn, afraid perhaps that I was being set upon by a rat or a student and what did I see?

"I'll tell you what in the wrong-sided world I saw!

"I saw three boys standing there, their pants down around their ankles. And in front of them kneeled three big girls having they selves a lollipop contest to see who could finish theirs first—no foolin', with God as my witness—a course I hope he was lookin' the otha' way since he obviously didn't have a lightning bolt handy for they nasty persons!"

"And don't you know it's graduation time!
Graduation to what—thug and ho? Well it certainly seems so!"

Miss Jenny Spies

Human Hunting Notes from Harm County: A Guerilla Patriarchy Citation

The Anglo-Irish Lords of that conquered land in the 17th and 18th centuries were in the custom of abducting women for rape, even the daughters of other lords, even as they raped and then sold their female servants into plantation bondage for the crime of getting pregnant. Their chattel buyers in the American Plantations shared their culture, their constant use of the word bitch to describe women of servile status and also speculated in African slave flesh as well as white slaves. Many of the habits of modern black Americans, including the ubiquitous use of the words bitch, fuck and nigger and such speech patterns as adding an 's' onto a non-pluralized word, rampant gambling and flamboyant dress have been traced by academics to the English gentry and working class, not West Africa, to which musical and oral traditions and other aspects of African American language may be traced.

Last night, at 10:45, on the #55 bus to Middle River, Miss Jenny, a school janitor, described an incident that might have come right out of the trial of Richard Earl of Anglesey and his kidnapped, enslaved and disinherited nephew, Jemmy:

"When I was coming out to the bus stop before the sun was all together down, to wait for the bus that did not care to stop—unlike this nice fellow here—there was this girl from an after school program walking along the sidewalk, face in her phone. She was a pretty little thing, I'll give her that, fifteen-sixteen at the most.

"A dark van with the sliding door on the side pulls up right next to her with two boys in the front and she does not notice. The door slides open and there is a boy there reaching out to grab her and drag her in—but he sees me and I fix him with the stare and he slammed the door shut in a panic and the van drove off, bumping into two parked cars in their haste. The stupid girl then turns to me and says, 'Did you see that, that van busting into those cars?'

"I told her, 'Little girl, you best have a care and keep your nose out that fool phone. They was snatching you up except for me being here. But for the luck of me standing here you would be getting hauled off to Lord knows where for you know what!'

"I tell you, men, the world's gone crazy and the rapture is past due for coming. It ain't no game out here. The Devil don't play and his minions are everywhere!"

The Great Society

The Wages of the Welfare State

Every material gain has a cost, either a material or moral wage imposed, from energy expenditure to consequences. The consequences discussed below are among the most predictable. While guileless libertarians babble about the Law of Unintended Consequences supposedly bumbled into by our executive and legislative rulers, the primal man knows otherwise.

By primal man I mean a man who has not let go of his instincts, of his native suspicions, who understands the seething quest for power that fills the souls of men who aspire to high positions. Men who work with their hands, who fight, remain in touch with their primal selves more often than those who have acquiesced to the simpering guilt matrix of sissy society.

So, when the most powerful men in a society get together, we know that they are among the most intelligent, not among the most stupid as modern myth would have it. Furthermore, these men understand the complex levers of power in a society that feigns democracy–which is complex indeed, as the idiot masses are lead up the meat chute of souls in the false belief that they are deciding the course of their nation, when in fact they are nothing but cattle thirsting for the trough and averse to the shocking prod.

To speak the whimpering tongue of mewing cattle, to appeal to cow and steer and align oneself with the rare bull, the masters of the meat chute of souls must not be idiots but men of genius, the dark counterpart of the good shepherd of Judeo-Christian belief. And let us keep in mind that even a good shepherd does much that is evil to his sheep.

When the most powerful men in the world–many with spoiled sons and grandsons among their wealthy friends and cohorts–they well know the debilitating effects that rots the souls of most boys and men when they are not required to sustain themselves and provide for their children. So, when the most evil men of my grandfather's generation joined in conclave to re-enslave a nation whose people had dangerously begun to think of themselves as free, they well knew the consequences to come.

On my last shift at work in a suburban supermarket, in a middle class neighborhood, I observed three child sightings between the hours of midnight and 3:30 a.m. One thing that you discover about customer shopping patterns when you work in a 24-hour supermarket is that families on welfare have no circadian structure to their day. Families that do not work, that only consume, live in a cyclic limbo, like zombies always wandering and seeking to feed. Latino, Caucasian and Black, all behave as if there is no beginning or end to the day once they get their snouts into the government feedbag.

Uncle Mike

A tall, muscular man of about 22, walks in to buy a meal. He works in some kind of security job in the hip hop lifestyle. His sister has four children by four men, who are well-dressed but starved for food and attention. He has promised them doughnuts if they will, "Shut the hell up."

These children, ranging from three to ten years are in their glory, like healthy minds released on a spring day from the confines of a stifling classroom to play among the daisies and buttercups of an idyllic parkland. Chirping with wide grins, squealing in glee, raising little voices in glorified excitement at the sight of the freshly baked doughnuts emerging from the bakery, they test their uncle's patience, but he indulges them with stern words as he herds them along, all dressed up in their Sunday best for this wonderful excursion to the grocery store at 3:10 a.m. He seems a good, hard man. But how will he, as he makes his way in the world, working the doors of nightclubs and making sure important thugs don't get shot, how will he raise the children cast into the arms of the feedbag state by four drones and one whore?

The system designed by a cabal of the types of men he would serve as a chafferer to, have already engineered their dysfunction.

Granny Gotchya

A former coworker, a woman my age, comes into the store with her manless extended family. Her once blonde but now dirty gray-tinged hair and her pointy chin, give her more the look of the English poor than of the destitute Irish, though both strains are apparent in her haggard form. She is not yet hideous, not even ugly but hard and well on her way to hagdom in her T-shirt and jeans.

Her daughter is a dissipated blonde mess who might have been pretty if not for a studied neglect, slouching along in flannel pajamas and flip-flops. The daughter holds the sacred plastic card called Independence as she walks stupidly around, either sick, tired or stoned.

Next to her walks a five-year-old boy, barefoot and in swimming trunks, having walked in from a lot where I have often found syringes discarded by local junkies. His T-shirt proclaims a tour of some rock band and seems old. He asks his mother for many things with a tentative voice and an uneager face, half turned away. She nods "no" in drooling sloth and he remains vigilant, on the lookout for something he might get that mother would approve of.

Stone-faced and fit, my former coworker holds on her hip a two-year-old boy, naked but for a diaper, wearing a close crew-cut like his older brother–both apparently of the same paleface father. As he reaches tentatively for something on the snack rack, he slides down her narrow hip and she catches him with that leathery arm and says in her gravelly tone of voice, "Don't worry, baby, Granny gotchya."

A snack is purchased for each boy from the "food side" of the card.

Two packs of cigarettes, one for whore and one for hag, are the main purchases, from the "cash side" of the card.

Broken Axis

Not a father in sight, as decreed by the system that bribes women to remain single while bearing children.

The Great Society, the welfare system with which the rulers of a democracy a generation ago bought themselves a Roman style mob is not the only ingredient in postmodern, cradle-to-grave emasculation. But this system of human degradation, in which the least able are bountifully encouraged to seek the worst in themselves, has provided the upward rot which has poisoned our society from root to stem, keeping well in mind that "society" is a purely masculine–usually martial–concept which is now utterly festooned with feminine cultic values. The spread from the underclass root of this toxic rot may be traced in the very sentiment of the beleaguered middle class, who more often than not, are jealous, angry and envious of these welfare slaves, rather than pitying them for the doomed souls that they are.

Indeed, in the supermarket business, it is very common for most "food side" independence card purchases to be made by a well-to-do middle class man or woman, who has bought a white junkie's card at 50-cents on the dollar in order to fund a fantasy football or office party.

This Civilization rotates on a broken axis–and the maw of Fate gapes wide.

Of the Night

Man as Sentinel at his Tribal End Time

As they creep and leap where the shadows sleep
In the Ghost Dance of their race.

-Robert E. Howard, Ghost Dancers

Last Friday night as night and cloud shrouded the parking lot lights, where trouble has come to me often, but has ever shrunk away, three youthful, criminal bucks headed my way.

I retreated into my dreamy eyed self and took a hard course to the left as they split their numbers, one to my side of the street, two to their side.

If this were a chalkboard diagram it would look like aggression, but it is not.

The flanker is actually having to take whatever message goes by mouth to the wholesaler who supplies these corner boys with the dope they had sold out for the night; the construction workers, retail clerks and cubical slaves who buy their drugs outside the 7-11 all serviced for the night, these boys are headed home and courteously give me a wide berth.

I am reminded of three crack dealers who adopted me at a drug corner 24 years ago and who called me "Caveboy." I was their mascot, their Feral Whiteman, a menacing and mysterious creature of their nighttime world.

As a man, I may not be simply a survivor to my people, but alternately a shaman–to the young fighters in my life–and to my little family and the women in my life, I am still a hero or monster, those who raised me, looking upon me as a monster and those who have joined with me as a hero. So, when not defending himself, a hero in his people's twilight acts as a sentinel.

The nightscape in my younger son's relatively upscale enclave, bypassed by the blight which has targeted my slave girl's less valuable real estate market further into the suburbs, has changed dramatically.

The next day I tell my son and daughter-in-law as they drive around the neighborhood, with me as a tour guide in their backseat, of all of the places I have seen violence, where I have been attacked and where drug deals habitually go down, directing him not to be caught in these locations and telling her not to drive past these locations. After digesting this, my darling daughter-in-law, who comes loaded with a fair amount of brass, says, "That's it, Mister Jim, this midnight safari bullshit is getting out of hand. When you turn sixty you're no longer allowed to walk and take the bus—we're driving you everywhere!"

It might not seem heroic to be the family sentinel. So, instead of imagining this decrepit author strolling through the hood with his thug-warding umbrella and sneak knife, imagine the last Pict standing above a clan cairn watching the Romans build their wall, or an old Shoshone warrior on a striated bluff seeing the tents of the long knives pitched in the distance.

Men keep vigil, especially as they fade.

The Coming Age

Returning Ice and the Scurrying of Men Who Are Mice

The current interglacial period, which has seen the rise of Civilization–perhaps not for the first time on this blue Earth–is coming to a close.

The Holocene Maximum was 8,500 years ago.

The Little Ice Age had its last wicked gasp exactly 200 years ago.

We have enjoyed and toxically soiled the Indian Summer of our age.

The last three summers have been autumn-like in Maryland, the year round rain-drenched.

The rain in early August has been almost daily, falling in sheets and buckets, unaccompanied for the most part by thunder and lightning–very unusual for this area.

Ishmael sent me pictures of him holding back small baby glaciers 20 feet high from snow that fell in Utah in June!

A mountain pass in the Sierra Nevada range has been snowed in until late July.

News broke quietly this summer that the so called global warming reported weekly for half of my life is a lie, that temperatures have dropped for the last 15 years.

The liquid face of the Lie is cracking and dripping tears of truth, giving up to those who would listen to their soul through their shackles of fear to taste the drippings of proof.

I believe that the pending return of the ice, the environment that European Man was forged in to emerge a world conqueror, explains the suicide of the paleface races, who beg colored men to rape their women in masse, who refuse to have their own children, who flee and hide and beg forgiveness rather than stand and defend as their ancestors did. I see the death of the great Northern race not as an extinction, but as a voluntary reduction of numbers in the face of coming scarcity and see also the exploding birthrate of the tropical races as the expression of a people with no organic appreciation of the arctic [this means bare land in ancient Greek] winter they are migrating into.

I see my mongrel paleface people and their cousins receding as the ice returns and then one day rising, great again, hopefully with some preserved insights from those of us with the discipline not to fight over the scraps at the Feast of the Damned, but to place a message in a bottle to some unborn soul.

Information Antidote

How the Body Politic Inoculates its Human Atoms Against Enlightenment

In studying escaped slave advertisements it has become clear that a chief reason for successful escapes in the police state of Plantation America was the growing literacy of the slave class. During that period, indenture contracts and travel passes represented the usual forms of identification and key tools for oppression. Flat on the heels of the era of mass slave escape which was prerevolutionary English America–staffing pirate fleets in the early 1700s and filling the ranks of disease-depleted Indian tribes in the late 1700s–it becomes obvious that literacy was a bane to the slave master. Not only could the "tolerable scholar" forge his own passes and indentures, he could do so for his mates.

In the Early American era, there was the danger of literate half-white slaves and the very common occurrence of a literate Irish slave running away with an illiterate black slave and playing the master-slave act as a cover story, for in Plantation America, before and after the Revolution, every hand was against the undocumented travelling man. This was a chief reason for the switch from predominantly white to virtually all black slavery, which occurred between 1804 and 1850. Ironically, the exclusive enslavement of blacks was only in force for about 10 years before the war that ended it, and throughout that period slave owners frantically busied themselves with preventing black literacy.

After chattel slavery was ended for adults–but not for child slaves until 1929–America found itself in possession of tens of millions of semi-literate to literate wage slaves. In order to control the behavior of these people they were set against each other across racial lines. But this can only succeed in semi-literate or sub-literate contexts.

Channeling literacy into fruitless reading can only be accomplished with a population that believes it has no agency. While this is the natural state of the female population and black men who have been raised under their savior government, there remained the problem of literate white men who believed they had the ability to chart their own course in life and were more than mere pawns or pets.

The literature that must be avoided is found in the following categories:

- Ancient texts,

- History as analysis or narrative,
- Subversive literature that places the man outside of the artificial State.

One need only emasculate men to direct them to emotive literature such as comic books, fantasy, political tracts and most easily accomplished, sports writing.

Eventually much of literacy was replaced by passive viewing which intensifies the emotive trend, reduces agency and dampens social aggression. However, at the same time that man was in the mid stages of his denaturing, the internet rose and within two decades, much of the literature pertinent to cultivating agency among remnant souls was available at the common person's fingertips.

With potential disaster facing the slave state intellectual tyranny, the terms of political correctness have since been brilliantly implemented. The phases are three:

1. Three-part newspaper article construction, with the form designed to cultivate bias confirmation of the headline–which is the intended takeaway message–serves as the basis for the system and goes back to the beginning of the wage slave era. American who do read have been trained to read like zombies, the actual reading nothing but a confirmation of some initial assertion.

2. Acute attention-span deficit afflicts most Americans, with few having an attention span regarding emotive subjects–with all topics important to the ruling elite effectively emotionalized by the media through trigger words that actually shut down information intake and bypass the reasoning process.

3. The taboo, the ancient art of enslaving minds by demonizing strands of thought, has been resurrected to implement self-censorship on behalf of the control organisms.

The upside of these means of eliminating inquiry and discourse among humanity is that, due to rampant emasculation of men and the toxic denaturing of women, that 95% of the population is so easily controlled through self-censorship, and that 10% of the population is militantly orthodox and able to quash the emergent ides of the alienated 5% in the general herd, that there is no real pressing need for old style censorship and erasure of information, as most will refuse to read or believe the truth. This speaks to the chance of truth emerging as a viable commodity in a post-collapse society.

The danger is that the emasculation of men is so deep that the feminine urge to control the environment rather than interact with it will win out among the minority and that their push for control will do for alternative ideas what the rise of National Socialist Germany did for nationalism, to render the prospect so abhorrent to the vast majority that its enemies will always garner broad support.

James,

The effects of mass literacy and the startlingly effective suppression of those effects are rich topics. I think the self-censorship you describe is not only imposed from above, but also a natural reaction to the overwhelming and often painful realities that await a careful reader. The truth is mighty, however, and lately it seems to be leaking out all over the place.

-Lynn

Lynn never underestimate the herd instinct of the civilized human.

Man versus All

The Hero against the Gods, Men and Monsters: A Masculine Manifesto for Literature and Life

I am in the process of writing two heroic novels, *Sold* and *Yusef of the Dusk* and am trying to rectify the elements of the heroic in my mind. I have done this more stylistically with the *Well of Heroes* project, which has already netted two volumes of commentary on the works of Robert E. Howard, all of which had heroic themes. These themes, identified as aspects of his work are:

Trails: The natural world, the actions of man and all of those other six threads of the heroic life, act on the hero to shape his form and test his substance.

Race: The racial makeup of the hero, his racial sentiments or rejection of same, and racial politics–usually exterior to the hero, who tends to an elemental worldview and is often an interloper–frame and impel the hero through the story arc.

Civilization: In a civilized setting, the constructed and affected world of sedentary, hoarding man and scheming woman frames the heroic in stark contrast–for the setting is his elemental opposite, best depicted in film by Tarzan visiting New York and diving off the Brooklyn bridge and King Kong fighting airplanes from the spire of the Empire State Building–to the unjust world, and also, in the hands of genius writers such as Melville, London, Howard and Wolfe, illustrates the corrosive effects of degenerate living on the human character.

Barbarism: In a tribal setting, the hero is tested in more physically active ways, though in a context with no less moral gravity than its civilized counterpart. The best adventure stories in terms of entertainment occur in such settings, tending to a less complex message and less compromised hero. In terms of character development, Howard and Burroughs surpass all by bouncing their barbarian heroes back and forth between the wilting embrace of civilization and the savage allure of the tribal life.

Dream: The inner vision of the hero, his education by way of dream, marks a return of the outwardly energized direct actor to his center, coiling him like a spring to leap back into the field that defines him. More than anything, dream, in heroic fiction and myth, joins the hero with the reader and renews his connection with his revealing agent, the writer, who must not be his creator. Of the many statements about Howard that this author thinks he would object to, the oft quoted blurb "by the Creator of Conan" would probably irritate him the most, as he seemed to be a shamanic type of writer who channeled his heroic visions as much as imposed forms upon them. In terms of the man entombed in modernity, dream is where we come to know ourselves and establish an inner distance from the filthy grotesques of modernity, as well as gravitating closer to our mythic ancestors.

Gulfs: Modernity accepts only physical gulfs, and eschews gulfs of morality, cognition and metaphysics, denying transcendence as a matter of first principal. Such a worldview, that denies the existence of horribly incomprehensible minds, of unfathomable evil or unimaginable gulfs in understanding, cultivates the fatally domesticated mind that asks "why" as the city walls collapse, that says "no, this cannot be" as killers sweep down upon them, motivated by such nonsensical notions as race, where the hero, fatalistically resigned to facing incomprehensible powers, springs into action.

Cataclysm: When gulfs separating the powers that buffet the tiny human soul converge upon the realms of civilization and rend it, memories of such events are only passed down to us through the ages in the form of heroic actions. The clash of man versus nature and man versus God in the story of Gilgamesh and Enkidu, of hero versus the gods in the Iliad, of hero versus gods, monsters and hierarchies in the Odyssey, of Saracen versus Christian in the Song of

Roland, of hero versus nature, monster and prince in Beowulf, all come at the clashing of nations and religions and lifeways that brought down tribes and civilizations. The hero is at the heart of our collective, moral memory and we discard him at our peril.

How do these themes align with what I have separately sketched as the elements of the primal man, or of the uncompromising masculine?

I will address these themes in terms of Yusef, hero of The Dusk, adventuring on The Red Sea and Indian Ocean in 1201 A.D., and Jeffy Tun, an enslaved orphan, sold twice in England and once in Virginia in 1678 in the novels attributed to them. But in life, we at the *End of Masculine Time,* must see the heroic in ourselves in order to guard against the final abomination of our world—not on the political scale, but on the personal. For a discussion of this aspect, or the expression of Twilight Masculinity, continue to *At the Feast of Souls* and *Gracespeaker*.

At the Feast of Souls

Why All Systems of Religion, Education and Government Cultivate Child Rape

Not long ago three Baltimore area people, a man who remains one of the few men he knows who was not raped, and two women, one a rape victim as a child and another who was spared from this largely because her older brother, and father figure after her father died at a young age, was a greatly feared man, spoke with me in various stages of agitation over seeing a Netflix documentary *The Keepers*, set in Baltimore, about a priest, who was also a psychiatrist and the principal of a catholic school. Witnesses, including former police officer from the time, came forward and were interviewed about the principal raping girls systematically, killing a nun, and granting rape access to police who helped cover this up.

The entire thing jives with what I know about Baltimore Catholic hierarchy of the day and police work, in which Baltimore cops from top to bottom, enjoyed vast and deep sexual access. I once interviewed the younger sister of a drug dealer who was raped as a child by three cops–one at a time as the other two tortured her brother in the next room.

I have recently followed an amazing conspiracy held in full view and not denied by its perpetrators, who instead attacked their accusers and even those who casually reported on their activities. These are the most powerful political figures in America and they rape children as a bonding ritual and for pleasure. The almost scandal was called Pizzagate and one should read Andy Nowicki's Meta Pizzagate for the moral implications.

I am not surprised, especially after the researching now ten books–seven published and three in the works–about white slavery in plantation America. The United States was founded on child rape and the willingness of the people of the Anglo-Saxon cultural sphere to sell their children and to buy and kidnap the children of their neighbors. Maryland and Virginia were founded on child rape, with a handful of men working and beating 95% of juvenile slaves to death in their first 2-5 years. In Virginia the proportions were roughly as follows:

- 200 chattel owners
- 2,000 negroes

- 20,000 whites

With 200 owners using about 2,000 of the 22,000 non-owners as overseers, and with no more than 10% of the un-free population female, what you had is a culture of child rape, a vast penitentiary-style system of dehumanizing exploitation, the sacred foundation of our nation. When wives were shipped in for sale, they were largely children as well.

We must understand that America was formed from a convict labor system and all such systems in our age have featured horrific and persistent institutional rape.

Outside of our cultural sphere and soon to come is Islam, a faith which sanctifies the rape of children. On a metaphysical level, I believe it is no accident that the two globalist systems, Mercantile Globalism and Islam, currently fighting it out around the world, are both at their foundational level and in their current form based on child rape. I do mean morally based on culture of child rape.

Get your head out of the sand and listen to Tom.

Tom was a U.S. military operative working in Pakistan with a partner. They were walking through a Pakistani city when a young boy carrying a water bucket was attacked, spontaneously, by three men, who raped him with a stick. When the Pakistani police showed up to set things right, they let the men go and then brutally beat the boy for the crime of being sodomized in public.

Two years ago, Billy, a five year old boy, whose mother is friend of my lady friend Megan, was brutally raped by his father.

The father was convicted and sentenced to 20 years after gross physical evidence and self-incriminating testimony.

Billy had his anus surgically reconstructed.

Billy will likely never be able to attain an erection because of typical damage to that organ.

Billy's father only did 6 months because of prison overcrowding and the fact that he was not considered a menace to society in general, only to Billy.

The Maryland courts–two of them–permitted Billy's father to fight for visitation! He lost, but there was not an absolute value that Billy should be spared. In the eyes of the law it is still of importance that Billy is some person or some system's property and that those property rights be recognized.

Billy is comforted by eating ice cream sandwiches and cookies but is acting out and attacking his mother, the remnant of the system at his scale that ate his soul…

Let's go back to the heroic circumnavigation of the globe, by Magellan and his men.

In 1519, during the Atlantic Crossing a captain raped a slave boy. The pages and cabin boys were slaves, kidnapped sons of husbandless women placed two to a ship for hundreds of years and subject to the depravity of 60 men cooped up on a floating prison on the belly of a beastly ocean. This captain was brutally punished and killed for his crime. The boy was thrown overboard, nothing but a condom for a man's sin, a discarded symptom of a sick culture that the pious Magellan had no other answer for but erasure.

Every religion, every form of government, every corporate system, every school system, is indeed, a manipulation matrix, a form of organization that subjects force to manipulation and is guaranteed by proxy force placed above the body politic and manipulated from within by the puppet masters of the system. My question is how does this not result in rape of children?

Once a child has been subjected to a system operated by people with so much more proximate power in their hands and mind than he has, and that same brutal direct aggressors holds the cords of manipulation, he is doomed on the carnal and emotional levels.

Our system—no system—has found a solution to this. But two boys in Washington Pennsylvania once did, and their pact is still in force as they fade into old age.

Faye, the woman I would marry and disappoint on my own way, but who still lives under my protection 14 years after putting me out on the street, was married to a man who ended up brutalizing her in monstrous ways. This was common knowledge to her family and even Tango and I, two brothers who played ball with her brother. Gaston, her brother was upset over his sister being raped and beaten, raped by men other than her husband, who he would bring into the trailer that she had fancied would be her little maternal island for raising her adopted baby boy, who is now the man that is my older son.

I know this story well and even now swell with the desire to kill the men who touched her.

My brother and I asked Gaston why he and his father didn't just kill the husband and he explained to me that his father would be taken away to prison for doing this and that he and his mother would lose their house and live in poverty–and besides, the ridicule of being a felon, a murderer in a society that holds murder–not rape–as its highest crime would emotionally ruin his father.

Later that night my brother and I recreated the heroic worldview that many a primitive tribe created in the past. If we lived in an evil world, we would place internal checks and balances on this evil matrix. If our sister, our mother–because we understood that our father, shackled by shame and the need for money to support his hostage family, was no better or better positioned than Gaston's father–that whichever us were better positioned financially would take over the care of the other's family and the lower earner would kill the offending parties.

This pact remains in force.

When my sister became engaged, her man was invited to dinner and my sister pushed the conversation to one of my more gruesome acts of violence and dumbfounded, my brother-in-law to be–looked slack-jawed at her and said something to the effect that, "So your brother is basically an insane killer?"

She grinned and hugged him and said, "Don't worry Baby. As long as you don't hit me everything will be okay!"

A man willing to die to avenge his family in the face of the unstoppable system who enabled his kin to be victimized and which will crush him for his crime, is the only solution. This requires more than one able man to a family and is the reason why our masters want a maximum of one man per family, so that we men will pay for the crime of avenging our kin by casting them manless and adrift at the mercy of the same system.

As a stop-gap for having the brothers that your socially emasculated father did not have, form a gang, a society, a brotherhood.

In the meantime read of heroes past and heroes imaginary, read of Roland and Conan and remember that they are in you, waiting to be called upon.

Gracespeaker

The Man that Brought Down One Chapter of a Multinational Child-Rape Cult

A graceless translation of Pausanius by this author, text broken for clarity, from his description of Hellas, Ellis Two, follows:

Consider these[1] not much. Unjust it would be to pass by the fist-fighter, Gracespeaker, his victories and his other glories.

By birth a Lokrian of Italy, who dwell near the headland called West Point, called son of Astycles.[2] Local lore makes him son, not of this man, but of the river Caekinus, which divides Lokris from Rhegium and makes the wonder of the grasshoppers.

The grasshoppers of Lokris sing like others, but across the Caekinus in Rhegium they are silent. The river,

---

[1] Statues of lesser men.

[2] The *–cles* suffix indicates honor. The meaning of the prefix *Ast* is not known to the author.

according to tradition, fathered Gracespeaker[1], who, though taking the prize for fist-fighting at the seventy-fourth Olympiad, failed in the next. Godborn[2], of Woods-Island, wanting to win fist-fighting and all-power-fighting before Thunderchief, defeated Gracespeaker, but could not take the all-power-fighting prize. The rod-bearers fined Godborn for his hubris against the god [financing a Zane statue] and also a fine to compensate Gracespeaker with a private payment for his injuries inflicted in the spiteful agony.

At the seventy-sixth Olympiad Godborn paid the god in full… and as compensation did not again fist-fight Gracespeaker. At this agon and at the next, Gracespeaker won with the fist. His statue is the handiwork of Pythagoras and is well worth seeing.

On his return to Italy, Gracespeaker fought against the Hero, the story of whom follows:

Grievedlord *[Odysseus]* as they tell, in his wanderings from Troy, was swept by gales to the Italian communities. Among these, he sailed with his ships to Temesa. Here a sailor got drunk and raped a virgin, for which he was stone-killed by the locals.

---

[1] The name of Gracespeaker and the river of insect song and silence may be supposed to be related, though this reader is of the opinion that Gracespeaker was his heroic name, after his deeds at Olympia [he may have forgiven Godborn, who was an egomaniac] and at the Wolf Shrine.

[2] Supposed to have been the son of Herakles, rather than his human father.

Grievedlord cared not for this man's loss and sailed off. But the ghost of the stoned man forever killed without distinction the folk of Temesa, attacking young and old, until, the folk having decided to flee Italy[1], the Pythian Oracle forbade them, ordering them to satisfy the Hero by setting up a sanctuary and building a temple and to give every year as wife the fairest virgin girl of Temesa.

They obeyed the order of the god[2]. Gracespeaker docked at Temesa as the ghost was being satisfied in this usual way. Learning of the rite he had a strong urge to enter the temple, not just to enter but to gaze upon the fair virgin.

First seeing her, he felt pity and then desire. The girl swore to marry him if he saved her[3].

And so Gracespeaker, armed for war[4] and braced for the fury of the Hero-ghost.

---

[1] Before making such decisions Hellenic communities would seek the advice of the Oracle to Apollo at Delphi, moral center of the Greek World.

[2] Apollo, via the Pythian Oracle, via the priests at Delphi.

[3] She would have been between age 12 and 15, having just bled her first. He would have been a busted up, broken-nosed 37. He could not compete at Olympia as a man until aged 21 and had been on the Olympic register for 16 years, had seen the world and was coming home to settle down.

[4] He was a warrior of the front line class, a heavy infantry man armed with helmet, breast plate, grieves, massive round shoulder shield, spear and sword.

Gracespeaker drove out the Hero and chased him down to the sea, where he sank into the depths[1].

Gracespeaker had a distinguished wedding and the folk were ever after freed from the ghost.

Temesa is still inhabited, as I learned from a merchant who sailed there. I also saw by chance a picture of the subject. It was a copy of an ancient picture. There was a boy, Sybaris, *[civilized bliss]* a river Calabrus, *[social division]* and a spring, Lyca *[Wolf, for predation, one of Apollo's cult names]*. Beside these were a hero-shrine and the community of Temesa, in the midst of these was the ghost that Gracespeaker had cast out, horribly black in pigment, exceedingly dreadful in countenance, his shoulders cloaked in a wolf-hide. The letters in the picture name him Wolf[2].

---

[1] Imagine the heavyweight boxing champion in body armor in a bowie knife fight in the surf against an unarmed special ops soldier. The black ghost went to the bottom of the sea alright, with an anchor tied to his ankle...

[2] This is the description of a war-painted peltast of the northern mountain forest of the Balkans. The men that bore such garments were the operational spearhead of Alexander's army a generation after Gracespeaker left the world of men. It takes little imagination to deduce that the priests of the Pythia [who was their ritually intoxicated slavegirl] saw an opportunity to have each year a ruthless minion bring them a fresh young virgin for their stable of child rape victims. Gracespeaker, as a man who probably visited the Pythia at Delphi and was familiar with the central cosmopolitan world of the Hellenic homeland, certainly saw here an opportunity to break a cosmopolitan cult

I heard another story of Gracespeaker, of how he reached unnatural old age and defeated death again, departing from the life of a man in another way[1].

*****

Gracespeaker, a worldly fighting man who earned social stature according to the conventions of the current mythology, used that status to snuff out a child rape cult with ties to the center of multinational manipulation. This man was wealthy and powerful and would have owned or captained a ship. He had brothers, uncles, cousins, training partners and bodyguards with him, all kitted out to repel pirates. A temple and staff, foreign mercenaries, undercover Delphic agents and certainly pirates for the shipping of the girl, would have been present. Brothers, you can bet the hair on Zeus' balls that a squad of peltests and a handful of acolytes were getting butchered in the shadows while Gracespeaker was chasing down the minion with the face paint and drowning him the

---

that had spread its tendrils to the far reaches of the rural Hellenic world.

[1] This segment of text was extracted from before the description of the hero-ghost for narrative clarity. Fathered by no man, but by supernatural agency, a man named for his well-chosen words, who stood against rapacious religious institutions and who ascended from life, not to die, but to live on as the hero whom Menander—the poet of the dying Hellenic world 200 years later—evoked Gracespeaker as the worthiest hero to be harbored in the human heart. 420 years before the birth of Jesus, we get all this, in the same language in which much of the Gospels were composed.

surf–that is how men get things done when The Powers That Be get too confident above the puppet stage, the bathe the shadows with warm, red justice.

That is the Axis that Masculinity rotates on.

The End

Masculine Axis Appendices

Go Tell the Spartans

'Sorry Sir, Last Stands are Now Being Handled by Social Services', with Hawaii Update

A lady at a party today asked me for a link to this story about the terrible abuse of her grandson. On rereading this I could not recall what book—if any—I had tagged it for back then, when it was written in 2013, so will include it in the appendix of Masculine Axis.

"…That extension is…three-six-two..."

"…Yes, Diocles…"

Dio-cles, properly Diokles, means divine [dio] honor [kles].

"How many Persians are there again?"

"Oh my, that is most certainly an OSHA violation. Based on your training and equipage you should not be expected to stand against more than three foes."

"That is correct. Now, before we forward your complaint to Legal Services, I need a few details. Was your insertion amphibious, airmobile or mechanized?"

"What! You marched?"

"Oh my, that isn't even legal anymore. I will also patch you through to Physical Therapy."

"What, the enemy is sending in fresh troops and you have no relief? Listen, Diocles: make sure your commander signs your overtime slip…"

"Leo who? I'm sorry, Diocles your connection is breaking up. When Mister Katzenburg finds out that this Leo—whoever did not have a landline installed at that wall—which I'm sure the Locrians did not build to code—he will definitely take your case!"

"You're welcome, Sir—and please, put on your sun screen. Skin cancer risks are grave in that latitude."

"What? Persian arrows are not FDA approved for sun block! Diocles, Diocles!"

Diocles famously quipped, when told the Persian arrow flights blotted out the sun, that the Spartans would be able to fight in the shade.

"Betty you would not believe what Spartan Inc. puts their employees through. Send an investigator out immediately!"

"Put Alvin on it. These guys sound like they have gender role issues."

"It's a spa north of Locris, begins with a T-h—just Google it."

That might sound kind of far-fetched to you. But is it, really?

The fantasy of the bravest Spartan having a smart phone conversation with a social worker is in fact a loose interpretation of the record, on my part, to make a point and prepare you for the following:

5/30/14 update.

Judge Kathleen Watanabe just sentenced Robert Demond of Kilauea Hawaii to one year of probation, a $200 fine, and a parenting class, for the criminal act of making his son walk a mile—rather than drive with him—home from school. Demond claims he was disciplining the boy for not answering him. Watanabe claims that traffic and child predators [our own Orwellian Asiatic horde] now make such traditional measures unsafe. So, if Demond loses his car, and cannot afford to pay cab fare for his little master, will he be jailed if his son walks a mile? No wonder we can't defeat medieval holy warriors with jets, tanks and robots.

Mommy Nation

A few days ago I was visiting with Gene, a hard-working single father, his son, a two-sport two-job 16-year-old high school student, and a group of older women. As I am known to be an extreme pedestrian, for which my sanity is often questioned by these good folk, I was told a tale that surely has my Grandpa Kern rolling over in his grave. Grandpa walked fifteen miles one way to work and back every day in the 1920s. He once dropped me off by a corn field as a teenager on Route #1 and told me to walk, and not turn back around until I got a job. Twelve miles later, surrounded by crumbing urban blight, I got a job and turned back, assured that I would not be vilified, but in no way expected to be complimented.

How things have changed.

Gene's son has been working on getting his license, but has to log more drive time before he can drive to school. He is therefore dependent on the school bus, operated by a contractor, who employees slackers. The driver on this particular route typically shows up twenty minutes late or twenty minutes early and does not wait on students.

Once again, a couple of weeks ago, Gene's son found himself stranded. Having grown tired of returning home and facing parental scrutiny, and not wanting to call his father away from work, he committed the gravest sin against modern America that a youth can commit: he walked to school! I was glad to hear this, as it was certainly character-building, and honestly, at about 260 pounds, this kid needs to shed a few. The walk was six miles, I think.

Did anybody pat this young man on the back and compliment him on an action that, years from now, if repeated, might save him from losing a job if his car breaks down?

Oh no. Gene was contacted by Child Protective Services at work, embarrassed and made out to be an abusive parent. He had to leave work—compromising his livelihood by at least the wages he failed to earn—and was interviewed by the protectors of his offensive lineman-size "child" who is diligently breaking with postmodern form in an attempt to be a "man." Oh, excuse me. 'Man' is now a politically incorrect gender-based term. I meant to type 'adult'. Gene was informed by the functionaries of our Nanny State that "It is against the law for a child to walk more than one mile to school in Harford County Maryland."

Let that sink in.

It is the law.

Walking, for which we are better designed than any other function a human can perform, is being legislated against.

What I did when I was six-years-old is now against the law for young men being scouted by collegiate football programs.

What was the response around the table?

Gene and I were angry. Everyone else was surprised. But, upon consideration, it was judged by the gathered mommies a terrible imposition upon the fragile child that towered above his father, to expect him to use his body for that one thing most suited to human anatomy, walking! Three offers from middle-aged to elderly women to give him a ride at a moment's notice, assured this young man that he will never have to walk anywhere again.

2,500 years ago a Spartan mother would give her son his shield and say, "Come back with it or on it."

Now, with the outlawing of masculinity and even physicality—a precursor to the hated socio-physiological disorder that is manhood—we have come full circle, from wolves to sheep. The American society that spent 300 years hunting down and exterminating the proud warrior nations that once ruled this land now produces young "males" who are legally barred from a walk to school!

The ironic thing is, in two years, this "child" will legally morph into an adult, who will then be sought out by military recruiters. If he succumbs to their appeals to his suppressed masculinity, and the bounteous offerings of subsidized college, and he ends up serving in a combat role, what do you think that will do to his mind?

You see, in our legalistic society, only one second on the clock separates a helpless child from an eligible war-fighter.

The Sedentary Subversion of Our Design

It [behavioral law] kills what it means to be a human being. But the people that enforce it don't have to live by it, because they have the money to live above it [the law].
-Monty, the "Grousing Sedan Driver"

Healthy societies universally recognize a "youth" stage, setting a place at the social table for the adolescent person, particularly the male, who must be taken from his mother's care and placed under the guidance of men. Our public school system, legal apparatus, and welfare institutions have been designed to take all masculine influence away from public life. Not only does the adolescent male never get handed off from mother to father at puberty, but our mother-based society mothers us all. On a gut level women of reproductive years know this to be true, and know it to be wrong, when they refuse to date men who live with their mothers.

I could go into an entire anthropological discussion here, but it is not necessary. If you are wondering what damage to our culture this "mother government" social structure can and has done, look at the back-stories of convicted violent felons, and repeat violent offenders.

How many had a father at home?

Very few, and of those who did, you will certainly find that the father was not a good parent, or possibly a criminal himself. Virtually our entire criminal class is drawn from large urban centers where it is essentially illegal for the father to live at home, for this would nullify most welfare benefits enjoyed by the single mother.

When the Amerindian warriors were offered government rations to come live on the reservation instead of hunting for their food, they knew on a gut level that taking a handout was the material reward for selling their soul. We, with our "mother nation" ethos, have not fought against the hostile takeover of our way-of-life. We have taken the handout.

A woman once grew angry with me for not accepting charity [a bag of food from a church pantry]. To me, in my anachronistic mind, that bag of food was the Devil's own hand-basket—the Dark Lord's ring. When I refused, she pressed me, and I responded, "I would rather starve than sell my soul."

She laughed, the pretty little echo of our materialistic mothering social paradigm. When I looked at her I saw only emptiness, in the form of that cozy nesting instinct that serves ultimately to bind us, and to wed us to the causes of evil men. This is what made Eve so frightening to men more primitive and masculine than we. She was a deeply wicked figure to the ancients. Her metaphor is all but lost on our current coddled consciousness.

Richard F. Burton, caustic social commentator and cultural apostate of the 19th Century, called the British version of this overweening mother society "Mrs. Grundy." He travelled the world seeking adventure, in order to remain a man by way of escaping a social model based on tea parties, domestic trivia and useless social conventions. Modern commentators have called the American version of this social phenomenon the Nanny State.

Well, I'm announcing that the fat old broad—coddling aunt to us all—seems well on her way to a state of total social domination that would have been the envy of Genghis Khan himself. We have been conquered without a shot being fired, 40,000 years of human culture destroyed with nothing but an appeal to weakness.

That, by design or by chance, is the collective world-binding genius that we bow to.

Banno's Babe

The Harm City Knife Fighter Who Fell in Love with a Cartoon: Fire & Ice Cartoon Full Movie – English

Banno was a total badass—a stocky Italian Vietnam vet who had served in the 101st during the Tet Offensive. When he came home a Chinese man he called "The Prince" hired him to collect debts in the States. One day I was at his place speaking to him about a black dealer he had tracked to a shack at the end of a gravel road in the Southwest [either Arizona or New Mexico.

He was telling me the tale of him and his partner with his two .357 magnums, one blued, one chromed [which he pulled out and showed me] rousting this fellow out of a bed he happened to be sharing with a white woman, for which these two gentlemen decided to punish him.

Using his underwear to tie one of the pistols to his face—the barrel in his mouth, his hands tied behind—Banno and whoever his less cultivated partner were, walked the barefoot man down the road kicking at his heels and reminding him not to trip because the hammer was pulled back on the iron popsicle he was sucking on—then he grunted, looked up at the screen at the picture of this cartoon babe crawling through a log, and that was it, the man was in love and out of touch.

I never did find out what happened to the brother as Banno was soon behind bars and when he got out he was pissed off at me for teaching his sons how to box...

https://www.youtube.com/watch?v=bZ8Yj6l-69Y

'No Small Beer'

RUSSIA'S HOOLIGAN ARMY (BBC Documentary, 2017) With Additional Video Links

Vasily "The Killer" and the Russian football hooligans, man for man, would defeat America's NFL teams in gang fights. I savored the whimpering of the sissy reporter as he decried the celebration of the Russian man's violent racial identity. Don't expect these guys to put up with Middle Eastern and African immigrants.

At 15:00 he lets the reporter know what's what.

"The current state of today's English hooligans is the same as your western culture and civilization, I mean deeply in the garbage bin."

So says the hooligan Chief in a very considered and informed vein, a man with five children and the nature to fight for them. The whimpering whites of the west may go without a peep into the gathering night, but as long as there is Russia there will be real white men.

At 16:50, in a drinking den, the wall has a picture of Obama and the Old Hag of Germany, with a notice that they will not be served there.

Any real human barbarian should watch this BBC documentary on a subject they are ill-equipped to understand, but are nevertheless driven to attempt explaining, gawking teary eyed at a place that will not embrace multiculturalism and the men that will sweep the streets clean of sissy invaders even as we in the Dreaming West look for yet another rabbit warren in which to hide from those we dare not face. The funniest thing is these Russian hooligans mourn the fall of English working class culture.

In the end this is an uplifting journey into a masculine culture invented on the ground by a people waking up from the drugs, sloth and alcohol that keep a man down in the spirit.

https://www.youtube.com/watch?v=k-2mMdGH__4

https://www.youtube.com/watch?v=Z9zy_-m0ktw

https://www.youtube.com/watch?v=hJnR5XmOZeo

https://www.youtube.com/watch?v=5l3ZSppq6fg

https://www.youtube.com/watch?v=5BKfVtkWCR0

'Brutal Impressions'

RUSSIAN HOOLIGANS VS UKRAINIAN HOOLIGANS

Many of the YouTube comments on this battle address one thing that bothered me a lot when seeing it, which was foul blows against the back of the head of downed fighters and multiple men working on one downed man.

-They volunteered

-They have safety officers, albeit they double as artillery spotters!

-The danger to lone and downed fighters is intended to encourage group cohesion.

-I have been in about a dozen group fights with weapons and can tell you that there is a special feeling to it, higher stakes. You do not go as hard as you do in one-on-one because you have to keep an eye out for the guy next to you and the guy that might have downed him.

-This is practice for real street violence and also a cultural cohesion ritual to bring back together a nation of men who were atomized by communism and alcoholism.

What is my ultimate opinion, if I'm King and guys want to do this?

Do it on a field, away from noncombatants. Don't kill anybody: If a man dies or is rendered unable to work, his team [the guys that hung him out to die] spends his death day every year doing charity work and the team who killed him pays his wife or family his annual income on his birthday, forever until you dissolve your team, which is hopefully never.

If you follow this rule, you can have your battles. But if you do this shit on the street you'll be shot down like dogs by the police.

I'd like to see this in stick-fighting with coifed hockey helmets to protect the spine. It already exists in armored combat.

https://www.youtube.com/watch?v=1lXt0vjbKsw

'The Spear Tip of Our Bloodline'

Matthias Waggener - Wolves of Vinland: A Tribe Against the Modern World

As an anti-social personality who takes a predatory view of life, I am called upon often to coach and mentor young fighters who are of the charismatic, "popular" personality type. My lack of connection to this way of life—as an unpopular, even reviled, personality—leaves me with a lack of reference. I am left coaching and advising from my perspective as the alternative ally and enemy of the Alpha Male throughout my life. That is useful still second-stepping it.

Listening to Paul previously, and now his brother Matthias, and speaking with and listening to men like him, personally helps me with helping younger men choose their path and develop their methods for navigating that path through the harrowing lies and thrashing personalities of the modern world.

"Their continued line of trash can continue—a can that all of these people can throw their genes into."

-Matthias does Eugenics brutally well

These guys are way out there, and by their own admission what they are into is only for the few.

Check Matthias out in this excellent interview by Henrick of Red Ice Radio.

https://www.youtube.com/watch?v=Y0xMQJ4sK-Y

'Outwitting the Twentieth Century'

Outlaw: The True Story of Claude Dallas by Jeff Long, 1985, William Morrow and Company, NY, 239 pages

Jeff Long is one of the American West's best narrative historians, with his masterpiece *A Duel of Eagles* standing tall in this reader's memory twenty years after its reading. For this story of a real modern outlaw in the conflicted American West, Jeff walked the land, spoke with the people where "convictions were forged in campfire" in his successful quest to tell the story of two uncompromising souls: Bill Pogue, Federal Cop, "with his faith in the basic decency of animals" and a driving conviction to enforce the letter of the law upon any and all humans, and Claude Dallas, a man who sought the grinding poverty of a nearly vanished existence in a bid to live elementally beyond the reach of civilization and its laws.

People fell out in a moral feud over which man represented what was right, true and American. But both men were much more than the postmodern man is supposed to be. Pogue was such a straight and decent arrow that he would not be able to survive on a city police force without being ambushed by criminals or ostracized by fellow cops. Dallas had a work ethic that would make him a pariah on any work site in America, unionized or not. They were both real paragons of a kind of mutually denying purity of purpose that could not coexist in their time and may not exist in our lesser time.

On one dry winter day at Bull Camp, where Dallas was practicing survival poaching, Pogue and a lesser BLM [Bureau of Land Management] agent gave Dallas a choice, be handcuffed at gunpoint or become the forever hunted enemy of the most powerful force to ever enforce the domesticity of civilization upon Man. Let Jeff Long take you back to the lost and forgotten age of the 1970s and early 80s, when men could still be as men had once been for at least a fleeting encounter, before the demeaning hand of modernity rendered them into caged and buried memories.

Follow Bill and Claude on their tragic journey through a land where, "The gorges are cool and repetitious. Scarce water keeps on carving the walls of the labyrinth deeper."

Thank you, Ishmael, for the chance to read this book.

Behind the Parable of the Masks

The Power of Myth: Remembering Joseph Campbell, March 26, 1904-October 30, 1987 by John Morgan, 2,315 words

As a writer on largely violent matters people rarely ask me about literary influences. Here are my top five:

1. Robert E. Howard
2. J. B. Bury
3. Will Durant
4. Gene Wolfe
5. Joseph Campbell.

I have read of Campbell's:

- Power of Myth
- Transformations of Myth Through Time
- Hero With a Thousand Faces
- Encyclopedia of World Mythology
- Flight of the Wild Gander

Below is an article that attempts to place him in terms of his morality—which we would call politics, since our morality is exclusively tied up in power and consumption—and does a nice job of putting him in context and linking him to other counter-culture thinkers of his time.

Interestingly, Campbell was an early victim of SJW attacks, specifically from a Jewish assistant of his, who was aghast at his not wanting to delve further into her faith and then conducted a smear campaign in which his vehement opposition to any notion of a spiritually chosen people was interpreted as anti-Semitism. It is only fitting that people on the political right looking to reassemble the scraps of culture left to us after the 20th Century should adopt him as a beacon of tolerance.

Another aspect of Campbell's work was that he decoded masculine rituals from mythic systems of knowledge and went a long way toward convincing men in my age group [late Baby Boomers and early Gen-Xers] that we had to address the metaphysics of finding our balls if we were going to go to our graves as anything more than the good slaves our fathers were.

"Joseph Campbell, the famed teacher of comparative mythology, was born on this day in 1904. For many people, including yours truly, he has served as a "gateway drug" into not only a new way of looking at myths, but into a non-materialistic way of viewing the world. And although as a public figure, Campbell mostly remained apolitical, evidence from his private life indicates that he was at least nominally a "man of the Right."

Read more:

http://www.counter-currents.com/2017/03/the-power-of-myth/

Flint comments:

Please clarify the statement "we have to address the metaphysics of finding our balls ". I'm having a hard time processing it into an understanding meaning I guess due to my lack of education. Thanks

The author responds:

That would mean we have to examine truths beyond our condition in search for our masculine core—kind of using your experience and imagination as a mirror.

'Engraved On a Stone'

Readings and Interpretations of Gilgamesh

According to my reading of Gilgamesh, the story represents three distinct tales merged into one in such a way as to tell a fourth story, that of man overcoming the world he had been placed in and thereby losing his way.

Most commentators address the Flood, which is a universal legend.

The portion least addressed, but most relevant to our postmodern crash in masculine culture, is the story of the Wildman. This story echoes in the legends of Herakles and Samson.

The portion most pertinent to the historian is the tale of Gilgamesh, of the King who symbolized the concept of Divine Right and through his actions even illuminates the, miserable plight of his servants.

The most sophisticated aspect of the tale, which I shall credit to the Sumerian scribe of about 4,500 years before present, merges these aspects into the story of Civilized Man, who, through his loss of his Wildman companion and their joint desecration of the natural world, suffers a disconnection from the divine. This story echoes strongly in the Odyssey and Beowulf.

https://www.youtube.com/watch?v=Kde-P_jffqk

https://www.youtube.com/watch?v=UrhpNRFFfJ8

https://www.youtube.com/watch?v=DmYPI42zgLE

https://www.youtube.com/watch?v=46Xst2do8p4

https://www.youtube.com/watch?v=8aWkR3QowdI

'Into the Rubbish Bin of History'

Generation Identity: A Declaration of War Against the '68ERS by Markus Willinger 2013, Arktos, 103 pages

The recruiting tone of this book is well-depicted on the cover. A masculine man with a strong jaw holds a megaphone at the ready as he looks from the shadowed space beneath the visor of his baseball cap at the woman next to him, who is regarding the reader with narrow, measuring eyes. This is an excellent graphic, encouraging the reader to progressing to the man's position.

Thrilled to find that some millennial testicles have descended from the body politic and immediately conscious that the '68ERS must be the European version of the object of my deepest disgust, The Baby Boomers—most degenerate generation of apes produced by this planet—I jumped right in, even reading the introduction, which I usually skip.

After being interrupted by a drug addict who asked to see the book and read the dust cover, giving it back, convinced it was hateful, I spent an hour reading and taking notes on this book and finished as I off-loaded from the mass-conveyance for dysgenics, pleased that there are still Caucasians with a brain who are not content with the soft seduction of their evil parent's delicious suicide.

Below are a few quotes to give the reader an idea of the poetic tone of this declaration of social war on mankind's worst generation:

"You've thrown us into this world, uprooted and disoriented, without telling us where to go or where our path lies. You've destroyed every means for us to orient ourselves."

"For deep in us lies a constant feeling of being alone, of being lost. We do everything to numb this feeling."

"You were egoists, and you divorced a thousand times without once thinking about what that would mean for us."

Willington continues indicting the weakest generation of humans in history, convincingly making of them an immoral corpse upon which to build something reactionary and decent.

Interestingly the terminally damaged millennial behind me, after accessing my web site and checking the bio, said in his yawning heroin drawl, "A boxing coach. I could have used boxing or karate or something. I've always wondered what it was like to walk confidently and then all that comes to mind is those kids beating me with table legs. If I had boxed, maybe I would not 'ave been getting high and going to prison, might have been somebody."

I suppose being a lone seedling in a garden of atomized guilt is even worse than the sissy, cowardly, materialistic upbringing I had. At least I knew that what I was raised to be crashed and burned when it hit reality.

'More Death on the Table'

El Fin de ETA, directed by Justin Webster, a Netflix Documentary on the Basque Resistance

In this lengthy series of very well textured interviews, done in the subjects' own language: Spanish, Basque, French or English, we are treated to a masterful example of the video interview. From 2000 to 2010, Spanish police managed to bring down ETA commando strength from 1,000 to 50 as the peace talks wore on. The interesting aspect of this was that the talks began almost 20 years before the final cessation of hostilities, between two men, one from either side of the murderous divide that has existed between the aboriginal Basques and the various invaders of their mountainous homeland over many thousands of years. The Basques appear as white Europeans, but have no linguistic affinity with the Indo-European races.

What remains understated in this treatment of a movement for ethnic self-determination, which is so abhorred by the West, from a terror-based struggle to one of negotiated alliance, is the uptick in Islamic terrorism in Spain, which was mentioned once but quickly glossed over. Reflective commentary by belligerents and peacemakers from both sides was woven a bit too neatly into a feel-good ending. However, the example of two men determined not to leave their generation's problems on the shoulders of their children and grandchildren was so serenely anti-western, anti-materialistic, anti-modern, that it trumped the smothering hand of liberalism that attempted to apply a false patina with less art than was devoted to giving voice to men attempting to achieve mutual understanding while remaining different.

One Basque militant, who spent 19 years in a prison system renowned for torture, would reflect that he and his comrades had fallen prey to the killer's tendency to get caught up in the means and thereby lose sight of the ends. This final note I consider important to the current nativist struggle in my country, to remain free from the mobs of thugs used to root us out by the soulless government. As a coach, I am constantly caught between my fighter's irrational urge to fight as a defiant expression rather than as part of a comprehensive means to achieve an autonomous—or more realistically, semi-autonomous end.

Bob comments:

Hmmm, I'll have to watch it. Immediately I'm skeptical of the numbers presented (show me one MSM platform or Western government supportive of separatist movements for whites).

One thing I'll say for ETA, their actions were never terrorist in the sense of attacking civilians (that would have been a very easy way to cripple the Spanish tourist industry). They targeted the Guardia Civil and government offices and officials.

They are a distinctly different people from the Spanish.

http://www.dailymail.co.uk/sciencetech/article-3229629/Mystery-Basque-origins-solved-Spanish-minority-s-DNA-hints-descended-early-Stone-Age-farmers.html.

The author responds:

There were only three interviews with ETA members and thrice as many with others. It was clear that they based their support on honorable adherence to their word and targeted only cops, politicians and paramilitary. I would say it had a 70% statist bias, which is low for a mainstream documentary.

'Born to Fight'

Bruno Dias Translates the Poem Galo de Rinha by Jayme Caetano Braun

Hello Mr. LaFond,

I'm Bruno. You may remember me from my comments on your analysis on the *The Deadliest Warriors* episodes.

I'm writing to you because I want to show you something.

It's a poem, recited in the traditional manner of my people. I was listening to it somedays ago while training and it reminded me of you. The whole theme of the poem is about someone who was born to fight, fought through his whole life and, even in the end of his life, will not give up fighting.

I tried to translate that poem to English, but I think I failed to really capture the spirit of the text. Anyway, here's the translation:

"Fighting Cock" by Jayme Caetano Braun

Valiant fighting cock
Rustic man dressed in feathers

Masculine Axis

When you drag the Chileans[1]
In the drum of a cockpit
On your warrior momentum
I see a gaucho[2] advancing
Bloody Fighting,
On the heat of the battle!
Because just like you fight
Face to Face, naked chest.
Also fought the old ones
On the conquest of this land...
And like you, without passion
In silence, iron to iron
They fell without crying
With spear firm in their hands!
I evoke in this blood of yours
That sprouts, red and wild
Splashing on the sawdust
From your bare chest
The rustic man on open field
With the poncho[3] made in rags
While scratched the shortcuts

---

[1] Here, the author is referring to the spurs used by the gauchos, and comparing then with the rooster's heel. The slang "Chileans" came from the fact that, at the peak of the gaucho history (the 19th century) the best spurs in South America were made in Chile.

[2] Generally, a gaucho is a man who lives and works in the countryside of the grasslands of southern Brazil, Argentina and Uruguay, often working with cattle on horseback.

[3] A poncho is a kind of garment typical of the indigenous people of Latin America, similar to a mantle.

of our uncertain destiny!
God gave you, like he gave to the gaucho
That never bends the plume
This male pride
That you bear when you're already a chick
And the difference I feel
Is that the rustic man, for good or for bad!
Only fight for ideals
And you fight for instinct!
And that is why in a fight
I suffer together with you,
When I see you almost dead.
Dragging yourself, broken and blind,
Like someone who says: "I do not surrender
I'm a rooster, I die and I don't scream.
Fulfilling the dammed fate
That from the eggshell I carry!"
And when I see you die while fighting
in your cruel fate
Without giving or asking for quarter
Rude feathered gaucho.
A little bit sad, ashamed,
A thousand times I asked myself.
Why I haven't made an effort
To die at your side?
Because in the fight on the life
A tie was enough for me!
Because I arrived at the end
Beaten, without beak and crooked.
And I only have the comfort
Like you, fighting cock,

If someone tries to bend my spine
It must be after my death!

I hope you like it, sir. Keep on the great work!

-Bruno

https://www.youtube.com/watch?v=J0fO4YsZ0VQ

Galo de Rinha - Jayme Caetano Braun

'A System that is Destroying You'

Varg on Idiots, Welfare, Russia and France

I love this guy's imitation of American dialects.

Varg's point on welfare has been made by Jack Donovan and I think they are absolutely correct. Is paying into an evil system so that the evil that it is may thrive?

As for his discussion of Soviet military leadership, it was even worse than what he described. Many of the submachine gunners did not carry ammunition, and the guy behind them did not a carry a gun, because he would have his gun to pick up, and so on. The political officers would stand in the back and shoot their men if they failed to soak up German ammunition with their bodies. As usual there was little difference in communist behavior from capitalist behavior at the top rung, with America willing to send men into combat in fire-lighter Sherman tanks, every crew worth the expenditure of an .88 round by the Germans, just using men to burn enemy materiel.

Varg addresses the red hair of the Irish in an interesting fashion. This is fascinating. The Pharaohs did intermarry with the Hittites, who are a mysterious European people who vanished from history in—apparently a migratory way. There is also a genetic and linguistic similarity among far western Europeans. I think he goes off the rails here, but it was fun.

https://www.youtube.com/watch?v=IF6fiaSKNNY

https://www.youtube.com/watch?v=75PcK_y0XnI

https://www.youtube.com/watch?v=o8tEQA17Db8

https://www.youtube.com/watch?v=TCWwa5Q0664

Baruch K. comments:

"Is paying into an evil system so that the evil that it is may thrive?"

It's a question of whether 1) you have an option not to pay, 2) the good stuff you're doing outweighs the bad stuff the evil system does with the money it takes from you.

"Many of the submachine gunners did not carry ammunition, and the guy behind them did not a carry a gun, because he would have his gun to pick up, and so on. The political officers would stand in the back and shoot there men if they failed to soak up German ammunition with their bodies."

This is not an accurate depiction.

There were some exceptional times and places where the Russians didn't have enough firearms to go around, and were in a desperate way (like how the Germans were at the end of the war, with units made up out of kids and invalids). Throughout most of the war, that wasn't the case.

For instance, in the summer of 1944, they launched a series of offensives that destroyed 25 German divisions in a week. You think they did that by having hordes of guys charging machine gun nests with their bare hands?

The political officers' job was not to stand in the back and shoot people. It was to propagandize the troops, maintain morale, etc. There were units dedicated to preventing desertion, unauthorized retreat and disorder, similar to the German Feldgendarmerie.

There were punishment companies and battalions where soldiers got sent for various infractions. And there you did have a guard platoon whose job would be to be behind the main line and shoot people who refused to go forward. Germans had the same thing.

A lot of this stuff comes from German generals writing self-serving memoirs for the Allies after the war about how they would have personally won the war, but for that stupid Hitler and those Mongol hordes coming on in endless waves. Amazing how many soldiers the Mongols (all 3 million of them) contributed to the Soviet cause.

"...America willing to send men into combat in fire-lighter Sherman tanks, every crew worth the expenditure of an .99 round by the Germans, just using men to burn enemy materiel."

Practically nobody during the war fielded tanks that could survive hits from 88mm anti-tank rounds reliably. A tank's job very rarely involves long range dueling with another tank. It mostly involves things like supporting the infantry in the attack or defense, or breakthroughs and maneuver warfare. In other words, working in a combined-arms team.

The best tank is not the one with the biggest gun or thickest frontal armor, but the one that's there when it's needed to do the job.

Meaning, it has to be cheap enough to be mass produced with the available resources, reliable enough mechanically not to break down, easy enough to fix when it does, narrow enough to go over most bridges in the area of operations, light enough to be recoverable by commonly available recovery vehicles, have enough fuel capacity, be powerful and maneuverable enough to go through rough terrain.

On all these counts, the wonderful German tanks of 1942-1945 failed. For instance, the Tiger's first battlefield employment was in the swamps by Leningrad in 1942. The tanks got bogged down, knocked out by the Russians, and then recovered by their trophy teams for research.

The tanks which fit the requirements were the Russian T-34, KV and IS series, the Brits' Churchills and Comets, the US Shermans (and Pershings towards the end of the war) and the Germans' PzIII and PzIV.

Tank duels are spectacular, but rare-you need the right terrain and lines of sight, and weather and daylight (if it's WW2,) and then most of the time one side does not show up, because it ran out of fuel or broke down, or a plane came by and dropped a bomb on it, or some asshole built a town right on the main line of advance and now the town is full of guys with bazookas and antitank guns that you can't see until you're right up on them and they're shooting you from the flank.

See: 6th SS Panzer Army in the Ardennes.

Trapping, Milling & Parasitic Malice

This Week on Ishmael's Do It Yourself List, With a Management-Labor Discussion with James

If Mescaline makes it to Utah, give him my number, will find him shelter, women, beer, Whisky, spring rolls!

Trapper Jake

https://www.amazon.com/Trapper-Jake-Korell/dp/B01CH39O3Q

This is a video about a man born the same year as my father, will send you a copy of the documentary, men like this were my mentors.

https://youtu.be/zcQXfTCedyo

The Passing of Trapper Jake

http://www.trapperpredatorcaller.com/article-index/in-passing-jacob-trapper-jake-korell

Grain Mill

James, this is what we used to grind feed for the chickens, whisky mash too, in my dad's time, looked similar to this grinder, larger size you could dump 100 lbs. bags of grain into the hopper, I was the kid dumping the sacks, doing this at age 16, they would back the truck up so you could work at waist level, would get my squats in for daily exercise.

https://www.lehmans.com/product/diamant-grain-mill/grain-mills?utm_medium=shoppingengine&utm_source=googlebase&utm_campaign=525&zmam=32933335&zmas=1&zmac=1&zmap=525&partner_id=bcbgoog&utm_source=google&utm_medium=cpc&utm_campaign=NB_PLA_AllProducts_GOOG&utm_term=shopping&utm_content=s2yssYyNI_dm|pcrid|54869971724|pkw||pmt||&&gclid=COjgh5z8wtMCFVIjgQodmpQE1A

Learned from the old farmers how to mix a balanced ration for pigs, milk cows, cattle, sheep, chickens, how I acquired my job in the feed mill after the mines closed, they could ship ore from other countries cheaper. Started on the mill floor, worked my way to general manager, rich folk moved in bought the farm ground, more money than the old farmers had ever seen, kids didn't want to work that hard for a living. I loved it.

Like you, hated manager job, working for lazy spoiled punks, so here I am, still working at a midrange job, envy you at times, would never marry again, never find women like my wide type would have to go south, to Mexico.

'My Guide and My White Father'

Mescaline Franklin's Video Pick: Stephen French with Danny Dyer

We have the postmodern, decadent, cool-Britannia, hardman worship with a slice of anti-white sentiment, but fascinating nonetheless, Liverpool (Baltimore's historical sister-city) is indeed a shithole, but man I want that scouse accent over the one I got.

Mescaline, I've known guys like this in Baltimore, but they were less racially mixed and more anti-white. I will be citing this in a future article. Of course, calling this Mulatto "black" shows that America got its one drop rule from Bitchtannia. The Davy guy, is a total disappointment. I suppose his mangina aura is put to good use showcasing the masculinity of the subjects. For the record, what happened to all of the Stephen Frenches in Baltimore is, they got shot.

https://www.youtube.com/watch?v=A9WvBpEzzAs

'Ice Pinnacles'

Discovering the Inca Ice Maiden: My Adventures on Ampato by Johan Reinhard, 1998, National Geographic Society

I am currently looking into sacrifice for a number of projects, predominantly Masculine Axis and my fantasy novel, Beyond the Pale, about savant in a very catholic world.

Discovering the Inca Maiden was an early example of creeping political correctness and is edited as something of a children's book. It is well worth the half-hour it took me to read it at the dentist's office. The modern anthropologists refused to make any harsh observations of the Inca practice of marching a young virgin to 17,000-plus feet, drugging her, and then knocking a hole in her forehead with a hammer or mace of bronze or stone. In fact, the author went to great pains to obscure the methodology of the sacrifice—the very thing that made it deadly and therefore sacred. I suppose this comes down to modern inability to frame the idea of sacrifice in our mind, in a society in which the need for sacrifice of any kind is seen as a social disorder that must be addressed.

Some fascinating aspects of the mission to rescue a dislodged ancient mummy from the crater it fell into, revealed numerous facts about the hostile environment the Incas brought their messengers beyond to:

- The mountaintop craters in the Andes are sometimes filled with ice pinnacles that seem like battlefield obstacles laid by some austere deity.
- These pinnacles only thaw when they are covered with volcanic ash, which absorbs the sun's heat.
- Two of the three mummies were struck by lightning, remaining nothing but charred bone within their fine wool garments. This squares with the Inca belief that the gods hurled lightning earthward.
- Grass was transported from below the arctic zone for flooring and remains 500 years later.
- Andean artifacts survive looting better than lowland artifacts due to simple inaccessibility.

It struck this reader that the climb itself to the roof of the western hemisphere had a sacrificial aspect, especially in light of the author's assertion that shaman took to the mountain peaks of the Andes to divine and prophesize, in my view the likely pre-sacrificial, primal origin of the practice of high altitude sacrifice.

'We Choose to Go'

The Mars Generation by Michael Barrett

Netflix is center mass for politically correct documentaries. If you want to know which way the world is tilting click there for your brain washing.

This production is focused on the NASA Space and Rocket Center in Huntsville, Alabama and its Space Camp, where nerdish children play with toys, play in toys and fantasize about a multicultural Mars mission. The prospect of man's return to space faring is couched as a totally non-physical pursuit—there will be no need for test pilot types in NASA's future.

The contrast of the armies of white men who made the space program, shown in old news videos, and this film's focus on multicultural inclusion and a ten-minute apology for encouraging the pursuit of technology pioneered by former Third Reich weapons maker Von Braun is jaw-dropping only in that it seems unconscious and agreed upon by all who are interviewed. White men have minimal face time in this documentary of recreating what they once did. The space program that made the moon shot is shown as clearly inked to white cops beating protesters in the streets.

The film does illustrate how politicians abandoned space exploration in favor of the space shuttle program and as Nixon put it, "putting to use" those discoveries resulting from the space program "here on earth."

The entire thrust of the film is its attempt to re-envision the future of space exploration in liberal terms and convinced this viewer that the U.S. at least has veered sharply from the goal of settling the solar system. Comically, the lone woman in the group of space students, the lone nonwhite in the science staff, are the focus of this film, as if the filmmaker is trying to sell the idea to people of color.

Ironically the U.S. is reduced to buying seats for astronauts on Russian spacecraft. Of course, there will have to be female astronauts. But the feminized space of color that must generate earthly profits—yes, this is the only acceptable reason to escape this ape farm—that this film promotes, is the sick American vision. The spectacle of an America female astronaut escorted into space by a Russian crew was telling. Humanity will be far better off with Russians on Mars.

'To Cure Me of My Fears'

The Strange Case of Dr. H. H. Holmes by John Borowski

The Netflix documentary of the man born as Herman Mudget makes for an excellent study of modernity's first casualty, masculinity. In a world of universal emasculation, in which male fashion stressed narrowing shoulders and wide hips and in which women found "a slight, elegant man" like Mudget "irresistible," was a world already turned on its head by the time Herman Mudget simpered into it.

Incorrectly known as "the first serial killer," [that politically incorrect honor goes to a black man with a hatchet] Mudget, known as the builder of his "Castle of Horrors" in Chicago, which was a hotel/body processing plant reminiscent of Robert E. Howard's *Shadows in Zamboula,* Holmes seems to have committed most of his atrocious mayhem on the road, using the rail network to crisscross the United States, defrauding and murdering as he made his duplicitous way.

Mudget was a whining, feminine man, who had been beaten and educated in the strict protestant school of his New Hampshire parents. Becoming a doctor, Mudget uses his profession as a means of building a fraudulent identity, dealing insurance fraud, elixirs and anatomy skeletons, the latter cleaned and reassembled with his own hands. His crimes were abetted by the unsophisticated urban sprawl and mass transit, and police reliance on identifying humans via the Bertillon body measuring method rather than finger prints.

An utter materialist, Mudget would have been a fine 21st Century politician or corporate CEO. In the end, he was nothing but a parody of a man, clinging to the very celebrity monster his greed had created. In his own autobiography he stated, "I was born with the Evil One standing as my sponsor." Addicted to erasing the identity of those who remained more human than he, the dastardly conman known to history as H.H. Holmes was very possibly imitating the dark art of Edgar Allen Poe, rather than expressing some rage against the machine of society, for he targeted those most entrapped in the very inauthentic moral maze that had stripped him of his humanity as a child.

'Boot Boys of the System'

Radical Agenda EP298 - Heil Heimbach with Christopher Cantwell

I remember being really pissed off when I saw Matthew on Vice's *White Student Union,* because he and his group were supposedly patrolling to keep the neighborhood, a mile from the gym I coached at, safe from blacks. I saw it as a PR stunt that was just going to cause race relations in Baltimore deteriorate further. This would not have bothered me if Matt was a Baltimorean.

However, it was nice to listen to his side of the story and realize that if only he and his friends would have been able to retain their sponsoring professor instead of having that professor told that he could not sponsor their union that their effort might not have turned into a circus. Despite the fact that I don't understand the desire on his part and that of other Alt-Right persons to argue with brainwashed drones, I did find this episode informative and interesting.

How many energy drinks can Cantwell drink—and he is constantly hitting the vape pipe? By the way, people that nervous tend to get singled out in shitty places like Baltimore, so it is good he's where he is.

The most fascinating portion of this podcast is at minutes 30-38 and the explanation of the White Student Union formation.

https://www.youtube.com/watch?v=Ea343UPYbSk

Genetix

Shep and James on 'The Shambling Shoggoth' Sired by Arnold

James, what are your thoughts regarding the two male offspring of Herr Schwarzenegger? The one conceived with the miniature Indio peasant certainly looks a more likely lad than the shambling Shoggoth sired with Shriver, although "quantity has a quality all its own."

https://twitter.com/PerennialYuppie/status/859081154191904768

Halberstram on Twitter: "The Bastard Snow is the true heir...

It's amazing how much difference a dame makes...

-Shep

Shep, my first question is Arnold's last name. From my very crude understanding of German, it means "Black-Nigger." If this is true one wonder why he didn't sire a son on Serena Williams, who recently won a tennis match while carrying her White Daddy's child!

Now I must look upon the Arnoldian offspring...

I particularly like the following comment:

Thorpe Retweeted Hoyt Thorpe

https://twitter.com/PaleoDeadlift/status/859183231375216640 …

"Kennedys must carry a huge deleterious mutational load"

Shep, I've been writing about the white and half-breed Indians that were so much responsible for holding off the rot of Western Civilization in our great northern land for 300 years—and now maybe men will believe me. When you mix a Nordic man with an Amerindian, both of whom evolved in northern latitudes, or an Irishman with a Korean for that matter, you tend to get a good athlete and outstanding warfighter. Gentlemen, what you are looking at on that bicycle is the closest thing you're going to see to Crazy Horse, the Sioux war chief, that you are likely to find today.

http://www.bing.com/images/search?q=arnold's+mistress+and+son&qpvt=arnold%27s+mistress+and+son&

qpvt=arnold%27s+mistress+and+son&qpvt=arnold%27s+mistress+and+son&FORM=IGRE

In Arnold's defense, she has a hell of a rack. In earlier age she would have been the plantation wet nurse for the Shriver brats. Also, look how well-made her skull is. She and Arnold have the same armor-plated head! The Shriver line is a degenerate strain of Melninonean* proportions. A healthy mestizo wench is preferred breeding turf over some devolved, gracile Euro-snob snatch.

*Images of Elrik of Melninone:

http://www.bing.com/images/search?q=images+of+elric%ee%80%81+of+%ee%80%80melnibone&qpvt=Images+of+Elrik+of+Melninone&qpvt=Images+of+Elrik+of+Melninone&qpvt=Images+of+Elrik+of+Melninone&FORM=IGRE

A Note from Lynn

On the topic of Arnie and the Maid, I was reminded of Rashida and Kidada Jones. You should perform image searches and apply your White Daddy descriptive nomenclature. These girls are the lovely daughters of Quincy Jones and some coal burning, gold record digging model. The one (Kidada) looks much more like a black girl than the other (Rashida). The genetic analysis is that Quincy has plenty of

European genes and bestowed more of them on Rashida's roll of the dice than on Kidada's.

'The Future of the Race'

A Eugenics Advertisement from 1919, from *The Art of In-Fighting* by Frank Klaus

What eugenics has become in our postmodern consciousness is an obsession with breeding superior people, with most interpretations focused on the killing of blacks and Jews. This view is pure propaganda. There was a bizarre belief in willful blood memory, placing humans as replicating ciphers. But there was also a more organic, natural attachment to the ideal of man and woman as font and vessel for family, tribe and race, which is to say a very ancient understanding that what we are made of matters at least as much as what we hope to be. The phenomenon of the hero is born and propelled by that dichotomy. As we sit here at the end of masculine time, consider, that 98 years ago[1] *our plight was predicted in the following advertisement in the back of a boxing book.*

Sex Knowledge Series

---

[1] At this very time, the world of high society was scandalized that the preeminent genius of the age, Tesla, was not interested in reproducing. It was considered a tragedy that he remained a bachelor.

By A. A. Phillip, M.B., C.M (Late Medical Officer of Public Health, Norther[1] Division, Scotland.) And H. R. Murray.

THE SCOPE AND OBJECTS OF THE SERIES.

Every doctor, every minister is aware of the serious danger resulting from ignorance of sex questions. Yet public opinion prevents them and parents also, from giving advice which would enable hundreds of thousands of young men and women to avoid untold suffering and unhappiness.

"The mystery and humbug in which physical facts are enveloped ought to be swept away, and young men be given some pride in the creative powers with which each one is endowed… the future of the race is in their hands."

-Brieux

Sexual Science.

Knowledge a Young Husband Should Have.

Knowledge a Young Wife Should Have.

Knowledge a Young Man Should Have.

Knowledge a Young Woman Should Have.

Recommended by Doctors, Ministers and Public Men[1].

[1] This was not a typo. The ad says Norther, not Northern.

*****

Contrast this advertisement and the opinion on Tesla as tragically sterile, cracked-up racial apostate, with the reality that numerous advocates for masculinity and racial awareness among American whites today are entirely childless, with no intention of having children and one sees that we are in the final verse of the race song—in less than 100 years, having fallen as far as a man can fall in relation to his ancestors.

Thanks to Big Ron for the loan of this book.

http://www.lulu.com/shop/frank-klaus/the-art-of-in-fighting/paperback/product-18754851.html

I'm Looking for a Masculine Tenant

A Man Question from a Woman Seeking to Home Share in Hard Economic Times

---

[1] The inclusion of Public Men with ministers and doctors marks this as a clutch point in our social devolution. These men were athletes, leaders and other successful icons of masculine expression, who were expected to have families and were—while sometimes celebrities—in many ways the opposite of the celebrity in terms of social context, not a proxy focus for the diversion of a neutered man, but an example to be emulated.

"James, I am a woman living alone in a house I can ill afford. In considering a roommate I'm looking for a masculine tenant. I have rented and roomed with women before and they are simply insufferable. Realizing that I am seeking to do this in the shadow of intrusive, pro-black discrimination laws, how do I avoid the ultimate horror story of rooming with a BT-1000! How do I go about selecting a man for a roommate?"

-Mary Ann

Mary Ann, what you most want to avoid is having young black men in your house. This is the best reason for not renting to a black woman, for she will breed and invite a parade of aggression-prone man-children through your door.

Place your home sharing ad like so:

No pets. No children. Mature men only.

Applicants must be employed or retired, 35-years-of-age or older.

According to Dante, the age of 35 years, in his reason for seeking infernal knowledge with Virgil as his guide, is the "midway point" in an enlightened man's life, at this age those men prone to awakening begin to do so. For this reason the presidency is not open to candidates under 35 years. This is also the point of athletic decline, a sobering occurrence for even meat-headed men. Men who reach this age, who are unattached and employed, tend to be very little trouble. Where women will always bring men into their dwelling, men are roughly half as likely to do so. When they do bring a woman into a house in which their mother, sister or land lady live, they will have already screened out the psychobitches, as nothing disturbs a man more than being under the roof of two bickering broads.

The most commonly reliable and trouble free roommates available are the middle aged man who is separated from his wife or the recently retired single man or widower. You can usually count on a year of occupancy and often more. There is also a security benefit to having a man seen coming and going and residing at your house. This is enhanced if he does not drive and takes mass transit or walks, because even the locals will not know he is home. My roommates generally have no idea when I am home.

Good luck, Mary Ann, screen your applicants online and be assertive at your interview.

'Playing Whack-A-Mole With Me'

Professional Victim Culture | Tommy Sotomayor and Stefan Molyneux

Tommy is absolutely right on one thing, that black populations and black cities are targeted for emasculation first is quite obvious. It's a good way of keeping whites from realizing that what overcomes blacks is going to get them, because the blacks have been trained to threaten and attack the whites and therefore the whites and blacks align themselves against each other for the good of the elite.

As Tommy points out, men are the target of the state and their extinction is the endgame.

https://www.youtube.com/watch?v=i-nzgizjhuo

'That Castle in the Sky'

Paul Waggener on Operation Werewolf Paths to Success

I am reminded of the Stephan Michael Sechi fantasy role playing book *Talislanta,* in which there is a race of genetically identical clones who rebel against their sorceress origin, by tattooing themselves and forging individual identities.

There is another parallel in the black concept of the government name and the street name. Paul Waggener is a very branded individual. Look at his skin and attire. On one level he is self-created and on another he is an advertiser in the same. The media he speaks of is Greek to me, but he addresses it as one who knows. He seems to be the right man to speak to the electronically shackled generation of human chattel.

Despite Paul's low diction and material reference he is working on connecting to shackled meat from a perspective very close to Oswald Spengler's transcendental scholarship. The value in Paul's approach, should you have reservations about his branding approach to life, is that he's speaking of using material means to achieve transcendental goals, as expressed in the current language of self-obsession, without being eaten by the side-show of self-devouring guilt.

In the second video, the positive/negative confrontation discussion is a very nice turn into aggression, how it splits and how it shapes you. If I could buy Paul's neck at the surplus Homo sapiens store I would—what a brain root.

In the third video Paul actually goes beyond Jack Donovan's gang model in suggesting that you must be able to cut it alone before you are worthy of intensive group inclusions, which is a very Amerindian view of masculinity and invokes the vision quest.

https://www.youtube.com/watch?v=ThmQCGxmMUw

https://www.youtube.com/watch?v=Bp12x3KcaXk

https://www.youtube.com/watch?v=HYqzzs2V49Y

'Why is *Survivor* the Embodiment of Evil?'

A Man Question from Sean

Sean commented on *Why You Are Food*.

Sean, the premise of *Survivor* was so cool—actual desert island survival—that I tuned in for the first episode, quickly tuned out, and have been afflicted by the sorry drama on occasion visiting relatives.

Survivor is nothing but an alienation contest that mirrors the atomization of the human being in the moral vacuum of postmodern society, as exemplified by high school clique politics and backstabbing in the workplace. The entire mechanism of the show as an elimination contest focused on petty alliances, feckless affection and alienation of those competent enough to make a difference, if one were in an actual survival situation, is a simple mirror of the deconstructive process that is modernity. *Survivor,* the show, is to tribalism and disaster survival what pornography is to love and marriage.

We Busy Seekers

A Leading Crypto-Blogger Encourages the Luddite Author

Koanic Soul

Thanks. I continue to read my way through all your Kindle Unlimited books.

Despair not of your impact. I believe you will become the grandfather of the reawakening of the white masculine soul.

Your growing circle of quality readers, despite near total absence of commercial success or even competent marketing, is the leading indicator of this.

We busy seekers of quality across centuries will restitch the corpse of your corpus after the copyright holder is safely dead and gone!

The author responds:

In that case, Koanic Soul, I will ask my son to press more Kindle unlimited buttons. I'm way behind on Kindle publications currently, primarily due to my inability to navigate the service.

At the Fireside of the Mind

Ishmael and James on the Savage Escape

Now

http://thezman.com/wordpress/

Good thing he never loaded grapenuts!

https://www.lewrockwell.com/2017/06/no_author/snap-crackle-pop-bang/

Before

https://highcountryblog.com/2017/06/16/before/

With the exception of my love for family, and woman, would sell everything I own and park my old hide in a small cabin, Wyoming, or Montana, alone, except for a good bird dog, close to elk, deer, fish, game birds, and all the creatures that I love and admire, grizz too, civilization, which is to me, pissing away your life on nonsense.

My journey through time, on a remnant of the beautiful landscape, of the west, seems normal to me if lived this way, would never be able to ask my family or woman to live this kind of life, they consider me crazed as is.

Would have my dearest friends visit, to sit by a fire with open beer, roasting wild animals, this gives me more happiness, and joy, civilization, or the state can provide, with the exception of my family.

I believe this was the inner voice that called me to invite you here, for the experience, to taste the life lost, living in your reality, I mean no disrespect, chance deals the cards, and I believe you have played your hand with exceptional intelligence and thought, we are alike in many ways. I understand why you write, because insanity would follow if you did not, but you owe it to yourself to escape on occasion, I hope your writing becomes legend!

Looking forward to the stars, at night, along the Greys, with my friends, roasting meat, sharing what only men can share, this primal force binds us, in a brotherhood few will ever understand...

Your friend, Ishmael.

You and Shayne planted a magnet in my guts when you took me to those mountains under the big skies.

I have to return.

I am experiencing a countdown of sorts.

My lack of fighting and an increased focus on finishing the many nonfiction projects, has left me tilting toward insanity. I had forgotten why I wrote fiction and why I fought and trained. I thank the hoodrats and pitbulls for reminding me. Some days I have to get drunk just to get a nap, half the week I don't bother sleeping. The only thing that stopped the spiral thus far was getting back to fiction, hence the astral weirdness of the Yusef story.

Been training to fight again as a therapy. It seems I will be the only heathen showing up at the heathen versus Christian brawl in Pennsylvania next month, which is fine with me. One forgets how much the body intrudes inward. I'm dipping into darkness in the absence of combative contact. Maybe your grandson will get to re-kill me a hundred times with those airsoft guns and purge some of this.

Thanks so much for inviting me out, keeping the portal open and doing what you can to impart your ways. I feel less like concrete than I did before making the trip.

Your grateful Lowlander,

James

'Addictive Distortions'

Wow, this Linh Dinh article is worth your time.

James,

Check out Mr. Dinh. Comments are well worth it too.

http://linhdinhphotos.blogspot.com/2017/06/doped-up-nation.html?m=1

Take Care,

Nero the Pict

Linh Dinh has crafted a heart-wrenching account of Everywhere, U.S.A.

I live on the upper end of White Avenue, one of the better streets in the Northeast Baltimore neighborhood of Hamilton.

Two doors down to my right a man deals crack out of an apartment.

Five doors down to my left a halfway house hosts a dozen young fellows at any time, mostly whites in court-ordered rehab.

Three doors down to my right, across the street, is a halfway house for older addicts and drunks, which coughs up a body annually.

I do not know the workings of this massive web of drug addiction, which employs cops, doctors, churches and lawyers in profitable enterprise. But the grotesque bones of its machinery break through the thin veneer of dissipating civilization like the rusted rebar bursting from the eroding concrete of this engineered meat-pen.

As an enemy of both the State and Materialism, I find myself wondering, "Is this leviathan of addiction, fed and groomed by its master the State simply the worship of material forms via the sacrifice of drugged souls, an expression of the drive to erasure masculinity, or is it a concerted effort to break the will of the American as was once done to the Chinese targets of the British Opium Wars?"

Mauki the Tambo Man

A Discussion of Jack London's Characterization of Melanesian Tambos

James, if you have read the story or have any response, I would love to hear it.

-Lynn

"He weighed one hundred and ten pounds. His hair was kinky and negroid, and he was black. He was peculiarly black. He was neither blue-black nor purple-black, but plum-black. His name was Mauki, and he was the son of a chief. He had three tambos. Tambo is Melanesian for taboo, and is first cousin to that Polynesian word. Mauki's three tambos were as follows: first, he must never shake hands with a woman, nor have a woman's hand touch him or any of his personal belongings; secondly, he must never eat clams nor any food from a fire in which clams had been cooked; thirdly, he must never touch a crocodile, nor travel in a canoe that carried any part of a crocodile even if as large as a tooth."

This is the opening paragraph of the short story Mauki, by Jack London. I first read this story probably over 15 years ago and the only thing that stayed with me was the introduction of the word tambo. I have often thought of this story since I began reading your work and your recent entry (*Reck and Tambu*) for that word in your *REH Lexicon* finally motivated me to find the story in my long borrowed copy of The Collected Jack London (thanks Tom) (I am not one of those people, I have only ever stolen two borrowed books, this one and another one, also from Tom; thanks again, Tom).

If the word wasn't enough to put this story in your sights, the title character is a woolly-haired, black twerp of a slave, albeit a Melanesian, not an African. London describes the systematic and unsentimental nature of the mercantilistic exploitation of the human and material resources of the South Seas, and traces Mauki's lone defiance of it. James, I found one of your former incarnations! I recommend this short story, and the above named collection, which includes London's well known works, such as *White Fang*, and *To Build a Fire*, along with many lesser known works.

-Lynn

Lynn, if I recall correctly Jack Donovan and his coauthor took a look at this story in their survey of masculine blood rites, Blood Brotherhood.

Generally, a Taboo or Tambo, or, as Howard spelled it, a Tambu, imposes a certain discipline on a man and imparts a power as well. This is similar to the Native American Totemic bond between a realized vision seeker and his patron animal spirit. Patron is not the correct term, but close and also, totemic imagery is universal in primitive masculine traditions. We simply have most of our experience—anthropologically speaking—with Native American cultures, which were uniquely accessible at the foundation of the systemic study of primitive humanity.

I am not versed on the Melanesian totemic system and do not know how faithful London is to it. However, Mauki seems to be a person who has defined himself as a tripartite agent. Where a modern American usually defines themselves according to ideology and material accumulation, most often in such a fashion as to deny their own agency, Mauki places himself in dire straits, in essence channeling his energy between the softening effects of female contact and the apex predator of his habitat, the Croc. The clam I take as symbolizing passivity, a thing to be avoided.

There are, of course, purely magical, superstitious aspects to placing taboos upon one's self. However, the process imparts discipline and a perspective in sync with the individual's psychology.

Ancestors to Virtually All...

An Anonymous Video Link

If you're interested in Neanderthals, ancestors to virtually all of this blog's readership, check out this film by Werner Herzog:

-Guest

Paleoanthropologists have waxed mighty sapient about Neanderthals being limited because their tool kit did not change over 150,000 years. I think that the reason for this was their inability to throw, which did not provide the imaginative linkage from spear, to atlatl, and from stone, to bolo, to sling, which were the converging points of departure to bow and arrow making. The Neanderthal tool kit proved adequate for their needs for a quarter-million years and only failed in the face of Homo sapiens armed with projectile weapons. Even so, all extant Neanderthal DNA is paternal, meaning that they gave better than they got for a good while.

They had much larger brains than we have. Large brains can have other uses, such as cooling in hot climates and sonar in aquatic environments. But, since evidence of Neanderthal ritual predates Homo sapiens, and Homo sapiens became intensely ritualistic after conquering the Neanderthal homeland, I must conclude that Neanderthal man devoted his mental capacity to something other than material tools.

My final argument for why Neanderthals are so important to us spiritually is the mythic prevalence of such creatures as Yeti, Bigfoot, giants, Wendigos and other northern forest humanoids. But most of all, is the fact that King Kong might be the most beloved and mourned figure in cinematic history.

Below, Neanderthal descendent Werner Herzog present Cave of Forgotten Dreams—The Paintings.

https://www.youtube.com/watch?v=W_seBLuIQjU

https://www.youtube.com/watch?v=DcjLW1YMhUY

https://www.youtube.com/watch?v=iNWvQbbPqf8

https://www.youtube.com/watch?v=yoSBMdAh_eY

'Cops Protecting Thugs'

Advance Show Notes for Lynn Lockhart

As Lynn has warned this here antiquitous, cracked pot that she wishes to discuss my assertion that police protect the very hip hop criminals whom they appear to be arrayed against, I am providing her with notes in advance, arranged in conceptual and chronological order, which will hopefully prevent her much queried crockery from veering off course into a discussion of strippers…

Proximate Force versus Proxy Force:

Moral superiority of the gang over society, of barbarism over civilization, general discussion of Alexander, Vikings, Cortez

Suspension of Dread: How low IQ disables fear as an inhibitor in large scale social settings.

Examples:

Uncle Crush
Big Nate
Vance and I
Haynes

Crazy Mark
The Pink Assault Rifle
Z-Man, Skittle and Michael Brown as chains of events expressing the suppression of proximate force via proxy force.
The BGF note

Thank you, Lynn.

The Dark (heh) Tower

Politically Correct Science-Fiction as Art for Life Imitation

I'm willing to bet that dindu gunslangers will begin firing with the sweeping sideways motion at 0:04 and 2:14. Which should reduce the body counts in Chicongo and Bodymore…

Shep

Shep, that two actors with such talent and presence should be employed in this towering travesty of white guilt and black martyrdom is astounding, a sure sign of the currency-worshipping End Time.

The black lead recently played a realistic role in a movie available on Netflix titled, *Beasts of No Nation,* about African child soldiers.

I like Mathew M. as the White Devil—sorry, "worse" than the Devil.

What we should not miss here is the continuing evidence that no literary mind has done more to erode the postmodern Soul, and take white men and black men further from their true heritage—and further apart—than Stephen King, possibly the most powerful moral carpetbagger of all time, with better command of metaphor than Paul and a sense for The Fall to rival the very Serpent, biblically credited with precipitating the first wasteland of the collective human soul.

I believe that Stephen King is the most important American of the 20th Century, having used his considerable talents to implant the deep moral sense in the American Mind that all that is most evil walks in the guise of those men who have done more to slay mankind's various monsters than the rest of the human race combined.

https://www.youtube.com/watch?v=GjwfqXTebIY

"The Unsullied"

Eunuchs in Combat? A Fellow Fantasy Writer Wonders about Emasculation in *A Game of Thrones*

I was thinking about subscribing to *Game of Thrones* for some cheap entertainment, and got to watching clips on YouTube. I've only watched the first season and half of the 2nd, and only read the first book, so most of the series is pretty unknown to me.

Anyway I was watching some clips about the dragon queen's army "The Unsullied" when I hear that they're eunuchs. I am aghast. An army of eunuchs? Are they really supposed to be a highly trained band of sellswords? Capable of slaughter? I get that Mr. Martin's world is a total fantasy with dragons and walking dead, but... an army of eunuchs just ruins it for me. What the hell is a beardless fat man with no sex drive going to do a man with all of his testosterone???

I remember reading about how the ottomans had both slave soldiers and eunuchs, (often captured Christian boys) but never did I read anything about mixing the two. I don't suppose you have?

I've suddenly come across my own answer to my query about eunuchs, though the example I have is fictional rather than historical.

Jack Vance's *The Languages of Pao* posits a far flung, space faring humanity. One such isolated world, the titular Pao, has a world-ruling emperor attended to by a corps of eunuch bodyguards. These are surgically and hormonally enhanced to be 8 foot tall, violet hued, artificially adrenalized sexless freaks. One specimen, when asked if he would like to be modified to be fertile again, angrily denounces the idea as the return of weakness. While reading I imagined them to wear a breathing/needler harness (Ala Batman's Bane) that provides just the right chemical cocktail to turn them into bulldozing juggernauts; however later in the book the entire corps of eunuchs is pitted against a rebelling warrior caste and is slaughtered to a... well not a man. To a freak I guess.

-Clued

Game of Thrones

Historically, eunuchs were employed in some military capacity, but never as grunt soldiers, to my knowledge. There was a very successful early Byzantine general who was an eunuch. His name begins with an N, I think, who supplanted Belesarius, who he may have had a hand in disposing of. Both were excellent generals. The leaders of the Chinese Star Fleets of the early 1400s were ambitious eunuchs. However, although Westeros and the world it is set in was based on history and British skullduggery, many of the elements that disturb you and I and other serious fantasy and science fiction readers I am acquainted with are the products of focus groups!

George R. R. Martin, who I borrowed from stylistically early in my fiction writing, was not going to have dragons. He was a vampire cultist of the Anne Rice school, whose early content readers encouraged him—talked him into—putting dragons in the story line.

Next, he waited ten years to write the final book, with his finger in the pop culture wind to see which way it was blowing, before putting out the concluding novel.

The HBO producers went even further in the direction he charted.

This took an excellent story that bordered on Arthurian and Shakespearean with deft modern twists and turned it into a focus group study in medieval fantasy soap opera. The end product:

1. Denies masculine heroism totally, maiming, humiliating and killing all the most virtuous heroes. The only masculine hero capable of growth is Jamie Lannister, who only becomes a reflective and sympathetic character after losing his right hand.

2. Heroines, good and evil, dominate the story.

3. Modern homosexual and Euro-African mixed race characters are inserted counter to the logic of the setting to broaden reader and viewer appeal.

4. The less traditionally masculine a hero is the better he does, with the story keying on the execution of the best man in Westeros, Eddard Stark, demonstrating the futility of masculine action, with his sons suffering the same fate in the chronological order of their traditional nature, with a bastard lasting longer than the successor and finally the daughters and crippled son being the final hope for redemption, the crippled son written to appeal to the sedentary sissy male viewer of our age.

5. White walkers are vampire-zombie hybrids, the ultimate enemy, making this effort a mainstream linkage from Rice to the Walking Dead.

Overall, Martin's A Song of Fire and Ice is the most brilliant piece of commercial writing ever committed to paper.

Martin is a genius.

The Problem with Eunuchs in Combat

1. Loss of manpower due to the 20-90% fatality rate of the procedure, as practiced historically on eunuchs of color, as the large black penis was more

feared than the testicles, would reduce the numbers of the soldiers and increase their cost.

2. Loss of testosterone causes weight gain—making for very poor infantry and unmountable cavalry—contrary to the thin, petite men depicted as black eunuchs in Game of Thrones.

3. Eunuchs are only good combatants in limited, stationary positions, such as guarding a harem, gate, or door.

4. That said, the Janissaries were effective slave soldiers because they were uncastrated homosexuals and had very tight—all puns accepted—unit cohesion.

Realistically, you have, in a purely corrupt system as depicted by Martin, eunuchs running the government and secret police and pack-oriented homos at the point of the military sword.

Dr. Jordan Peterson?

Travolta Wants to Know What the Harm City Crackpot Thinks

I might have missed it on your blog, but have you been listening to the podcasts and interviews with Dr. Jordan Peterson? If so, what's your thinking about this guy?

-Travolta

Travolta, thanks for the heads up. I don't search the net outside of slavery research and am dependent on readers such as yourself. Being about 20 hours short of being able to comment intelligently on Peterson's work, I do know where I will slot his material, in the Masculine Axis. Since 2005, when completing the research for *The First Boxers* and *The Gods of Boxing,* I have believed that the relative lack of masculinity in modern times, beginning in the late 1800s, is closely related to the diminishment of such sacred traditions as vision quests, prize fighting [these began as sacral rites], hunting [sacred undertakings through most of human history], warriorhood giving way to soldiering and the reduction in mythic literature free of gross exposition and womanly sensibilities.

I have, more recently, from a deistic perspective, following Aristotle, been astounded, by self-proclaimed Aristotle disciple Stefan Molyneux, first claiming atheism as the only rational worldview, while discarding Aristotle's deistic vision of God as "The Cause Uncaused" or "the Unmoved Mover," a view Darwin was also aligned with, and then to see him, as he began stumping for the Trump campaign, miraculously become a Christian! This latter day conversion was suspiciously inline with the Canadian Socrates' desperate scramble to maintain his earnings curve in the face of rampant censorship. Interestingly, concurrent with Molyneux's new religious persona, is an overt masculine gimmickry, which ill-fits his formerly whining "men's rights" stance. For this reason, I searched Molyneux, and sure enough he has scored an interview with Peterson...

Above all, I am fascinated that the mental health gurus are beginning to suck up to the traditional religious notions they railed against for centuries, seemingly horrified by the fact that their "pure" appeal to reason in the absence of the sacred has turned hierarchal and media manipulation of the collective mind into a religion more monstrous than anything the Romans, Aztecs, Huns or Sudanese ever cleaved to in their various ancient ways.

I am entertained, intrigued and hopeful.

https://jordanbpeterson.com/jordan-b-peterson-podcast/

https://www.youtube.com/watch?v=f-wWBGo6a2w

https://www.youtube.com/watch?v=1kdnmT_7gLE

Postmodern NeoMarxism: Diagnosis and Cure

https://www.youtube.com/watch?v=s4c-jOdPTN8&t=884s

Joe Rogan Experience #958 - Jordan Peterson

https://www.youtube.com/watch?v=USg3NR76XpQ

Maps of Meaning: The Architecture of Belief

Made in the USA
Coppell, TX
18 October 2021